Five Minutes
to Mindfulness—Kids

Because Being Yourself Needn't Take Time

Dr. Ashleigh Stewart Msc.D.

BALBOA.
PRESS
A DIVISION OF HAY HOUSE

Balboa Press books may be ordered through booksellers or by contacting:

Balboa Press
A Division of Hay House
1663 Liberty Drive
Bloomington, IN 47403
www.balboapress.com
1 (877) 407-4847

Because of the dynamic nature of the Internet, any web addresses or links contained in this book may have changed since publication and may no longer be valid. The views expressed in this work are solely those of the author and do not necessarily reflect the views of the publisher, and the publisher hereby disclaims any responsibility for them.

The author of this book does not dispense medical advice or prescribe the use of any technique as a form of treatment for physical, emotional, or medical problems without the advice of a physician, either directly or indirectly. The intent of the author is only to offer information of a general nature to help you in your quest for emotional and spiritual well-being. In the event you use any of the information in this book for yourself, which is your constitutional right, the author and the publisher assume no responsibility for your actions.

Any people depicted in stock imagery provided by Thinkstock are models, and such images are being used for illustrative purposes only. Certain stock imagery © Thinkstock.

Print information available on the last page.

ISBN: 978-1-5043-8282-3 (sc)
ISBN: 978-1-5043-8284-7 (hc)
ISBN: 978-1-5043-8283-0 (e)

Library of Congress Control Number: 2017909789

Balboa Press rev. date: 06/22/2017

Contents

'Five Minutes to Mindfulness is a gift for any parent or teacher who is searching for alternative ways of simplifying the lives of the children in their care or guidance. Dr. Ashleigh Stewart's deep sense of compassion and care for children is revealed, and shines through in every page of this book. She writes with the wisdom, honesty, conviction and compassion that only a true visionary and transformational leader could possess. This book is a must-read for adults who are searching for ways to support their children that are beyond the societal 'norm'.'

- Joseph Ghabi B.Msc. Bestselling Author and Founder of The Free Spirit Centre

Never before in the history of time have we seen the masses suffering from chronic stress, distress, fear and anxiety.

Unfortunately this is now being passed down to our children. As humanity faces a global shift of consciousness into one with a greater effect of the mind on the body, and the body on the mind, it has never been so urgent for the younger generations to learn to understand the practice of yoga and mindfulness, and how to implement it into their daily routine to help them cope with the struggles they face daily at school and at home.

Yoga offers a holistic body/mind/spirit system which enables us to tap into our body's own intelligent technology within. This technology is like an inner pharmacy which can help us to balance, and maintain good health in the body, mind and spirit as one. However, it can only be accessed through the taming of the mind from the daily mental chatter we experience as a result of our stresses.

In this book, Dr. Ashleigh has defined and outlined simple yet effective strategies that parents and teachers alike can teach their children to use both in group settings, or individually one on one.

As an internationally renowned and well respected leader in our global Yoga community I myself would recommend this book to anyone who is looking for simple, yet effective ways to bring their children up mindfully, with a strong sense of self-awareness and an understanding of the power of their mind body and emotions.

- DrMadan Bali PH.D. Internationally renowned teacher, speaker and founder of Yoga Bliss Training and Research Institute Montreal.

"Dr Ashleigh has written a short, succinct guide to helping your child face the world with greater confidence and with exercises that will be fun and useful for the child for all its life. If every parent displayed Ashleigh's conscientiousness and thoughtfulness about child-rearing and equaled her depth of affection we could all celebrate a new generation of well-grounded people.

Dr Ashleigh's blend of mindfulness programs with ancient yogic practices is right on the money and now every parent has a winning formula to reach out with intimacy and a profound way of sharing which I believe may imbue each child with a strong value system. The child, as beneficiary of these exercises, will be emboldened by the wise mother's love and concern for the mental well-being of her cherished children.

Work with Ashleigh and your children and witness the encouraging results."

Harry Langen, author.

Preface

"Keep me away from the wisdom which does not cry, the philosophy which does not laugh and the greatness which does not bow before children." -Kahlil Gibran

I AM WRITING this book to offer insight in light of the many struggles our children are going through in today's fast-pacedfast pacedand hectic society. The intention of this book is to offer awareness combined with a practical tool to help adults better understand children.

When you understand children, it means you can help them to get to know themselves mentally and emotionally, which will in turn help them to better understand how they relate both with others and the world around them. It is my belief that when a child knows himself deeply, with a strong sense of self-power, confidence, emotional intelligence and integrity, the better he will be prepared to lead a successful and happy life imbued with purpose and fulfillment. I also believe that when a child is self-aware it helps to reduce the likelihood of the development of behavioral disorders, depression, anxiety and mental health issues that children are so frequently being diagnosed with these days.

Children aside for a moment, in a challenging societymany adults too mayhave a hard time knowing who they are and what they truly want. I believe when someone does not really know who they are, they cannot feel a true sense of fulfillment and purpose in life. We have been raised to believe that our sole purpose is to fit into a 'one size fits all system' that demands us to fit in at school; memorize facts on subjects; get a job; pay taxes;accumulate as much money as possible; climb the corporate ladder; have more kids, and then train them to do the same thing.It is unreasonable to slot anyone into a system that isn't designed to suit everyone and then expect them to function at full potential, thriving with a sense of authentic fulfillment. It is also unreasonable to claim they are disordered or dysfunctional as a result.

Many of us are starting to awaken to the idea that it is okay to livea bit differently, and that it is okay to be creative and work with your own ideas outside of the cookie-cutter existence we are so accustomed to. That being said, where do we begin to change things for the betterment of our world? The best way to begin is with a blank canvas: our children!

On that note, I'd like to talk about my own young daughter Tiffany. Tiffany has demonstrated that she is smart, observant, sensitive and intelligent beyond ways in which our traditional education system currently supports. As a result of this, my daughter has suffered an array of different troubling symptoms and reactions as she has never really had her needs fulfilled in the classroom because she has never been able to approach learning in ways that suit her unique character and personality, and as a result has never been seen for who she really is.

How the school system affects our children and how they see themselves growing up is a critical component of a child's mental, social, emotional and psychological development. The majority of time spent by children is in the classroom under the influence of their teachers and peers in an educational system and here it is crucial that the system supports our child's best interests socially, emotionally and psychologically, not just intellectually. The word 'holistic' comes to mind.

In my own experience with my daughter, I started to notice that when school was in, my daughter would experience anxiety, low self-esteem, and lack of self-confidence, bad dreams, bed-wetting, negative self-talk and a bad attitude. She was not responding well to the traditional classroom which is over-crowded with mixed grade kids ranging between the ages of seven to nine years old, a ridiculous age gap within which kids are expected to learn at the same pace.This is the worrisome situation kids in the system are immersed in these days.

Unfortunately, my daughter had been in a mixed grade classroom with close to 30 kids in attendance since grade one. I feel that the expectations on a child to perform at a level which is geared to support the learning of other children who are one or two years older than they are is simply ludicrous. Later after some intervention and support from her reading recovery teacher, fate stepped in and she was given the opportunity to join in 'SELC' a 'Social, Emotional Learning Center' program at a different school. The SELC class consisted of only ten children, three teachers and a therapy dog and the focus was on mindfulness, emotional intelligence, emotional regulation and self-awareness and respect for others. I had the opportunity to go and teach yoga to the kids in this group and the experience was amazing.

As a parent and a teacher, I feel that the lessons that are being taught in the SELC programs are the tools that children need to learn first before we immerse them into a demanding school system as they will be better equipped to handle the challenges of the day-to-day curriculum with a stronger sense of self awareness and emotional intelligence to help regulate feelings of fear, anxiety and stress.

Although the volume of children being diagnosed with learning and behavioral disorders is ever increasing, and at younger ages too, I truly believe that children these days are not dysfunctional, they just do not have all the tools they need to help them adapt to the different learning styles and personalities that a 'one size fits all' learning experience expects from them.

My daughter went to SELC every day from 11 to 3.30pm for 15 weeks and during this time I watched my child slowly transform into the more relaxed, happy, and creative child she actually is. I was blown away as I started to hear her humming to herself periodically, laughing, smiling to herself during the day and we were finally able to have normal conversations that didn't involve aggravation and resistance. This all took time, not medication. There was no medical diagnosis involved in this, simply time. Patience, love, understanding and a different approach to learning which allowed her to know, and be herself.

From the perspective of being her parent, I can say that handling this situation forced me to work on myself too. I had to work hard to slow down, breathe and let myself be in the moment with her to intuitively feel what was going on. Doing so allowed me to then become selfless by letting go of my own expectation of how I thought she ought to be feeling and acting by listening to her instead of reacting with judgment. When I was present with her I was able to guide her through her feelings and help her understand a situation calmly instead of her becoming confused and angry. I allowed my daughter to be herself and not the girl I expected her to be and the energy of our interactions changed from being strained, 'high energy' situations to ones of peace, trust and consideration.

Dealing with my daughter became my opportunity for my own five minutes for mindfulness when I slowed down and spent time being present in the moment with her. Spending five minutes of mindfulness anytime of the day with my both of my children has allowed me to see them for who they really are, recognize how they are feeling and guide them toward being in a place of peace and understanding instead of fear and confusion. Now, I can truly say we are able to sit in a place of love with an authentic connection which is based on trust and acceptance as we grow together through understanding each other. This realization is the fuel behind what inspired be to write this book. I hope you are able to find the same meeting place of peace with your own child so you can both flourish and grow in love and patience together.

Chapter 1

Why Five Minutes to Mindfulness?

"Because being yourself needn't take time!" – Dr. Ashleigh Stewart

I WAS COMPELLED to write this book called 'Five Minutes to Mindfulness' for Kids because as a busy mother I know that it can be hard to fit any new programs into an already busy work/life/family routine. Many of the parents I have begun working with in a program of mindfulness for their children claim that they are apprehensive to try it out because they do not have time for anything as it is.

I am here to tell you that the beauty of mindfulness and getting to know who your children really are needn't take time. I have studied many disciplines and practices in spirituality, holistic science, healthcare and even psychology and after dipping my toe into them all I decided to delve deeply into studying the practice of yoga and mindfulness because of its simplicity. Yoga is a system of which connects perfectly with a mindfulness practice as yoga exercises are all rooted in actions that involve being in the present moment. The exercises outlined later in the book are derived

1

mainly from the school of hatha yoga, and the majority of them have been designed to fit nicely into your already hectic routine without fuss!

The exercises in this book are fun and creative, many of them are designed to be done in groups so they offer a great opportunity for siblings and family members to bond, build respect and develop trust and friendship.

The long term goal at the end of this practice is that this work becomes so routine that it becomes a way of life, so much so that its practice becomes a natural way of being and a great foundation for children to build a sense of who they are and how they relate and respond to the world around them as they are growing up.

Chapter 2

What's Behind their Behavior?

"We think of children as vulnerable. In my experience, they're giants. Their bodies and souls are amazingly resilient. What we often mistake for fragility is their openness." - Fred Epstein

CHILDREN AND ADULTS function very differently psychologically; however, children are not too difficult to understand if we are able to meet them at their level mentally and emotionally. This means letting go of our pre-conceived notions of how we as adults think they ought to think, feel and behave.

An adult who grew up as a child who was misunderstood may find it hard to guide a child to discover his own self-awareness, having had no concept of this of his own during childhood. On the other hand, growing up feeling misunderstood might motivate an adult more to try to help his child find himself. Either way, as adults we can make it our goal to work on our own personal development as we endeavor to raise children. This way we will feel confident that we are doing our best to be the best parents we can be. We are never perfect as parents, nor do we have all the answers, yet at least we can rest assured we are doing our best to be the most consciously aware adult we can be to help guide our children through the world and out into life feeling self-assured, and equipped with confidence.

Communicating with children can be tricky, especially during challenging 'high energy' situations such as tantrums, melt-downs or anxiety attacks triggered by common day-to-day events such as hair-washing, difficult homework or refusing to go to bed. During such times, it is important to consider the fact that adults have the ability to understand their own feelings and have the intelligence to articulate them. Children are still developing the capacity to intelligently articulate their feelings, which can be frustrating for them. Because children do not have the same capacity to communicate their thoughts and feelings as adults do, behavior becomes their communication tool. When a misunderstood child is around an adult who does not appear to understand him, and is not listening to what he is trying to say, he uses his best means of getting attention to what he is trying to communicate, his behavior.

Unfortunately negative behavior tends to get attention at a faster rate of response than any other means for kids, and the worse the behavior the bigger the response as the child will receive more attention. It is because of this that I believe much of the diagnosis of behavioral disorders such as ODD and ADHD is misplaced. It is not these alleged mental disorders that is the problem. The 'disorder'here is in the way the child is perceived by the adults around him.

Here is a list of age appropriate developmental challenges which could be behind why children use negative behavior as a means of communication:

- Due to their lack of maturity, children may not understand the array of emotions they are feeling, and why they are feeling them.
- Children have a limited use of vocabulary.
- Children may be unable to identify and connect words with emotions due to the factors mentioned above.
- Limited capacity for self-expression as a result of rigid guidelines and expectations from either parents or teachers at school.
- due to a lack of self-awareness, children may feel a flawed sense of identity due to projected pressure and expectations of adults
- Children are very sensitive to emotional energies in the environment which is natural during youth. Stressed-out and anxious adults pass the same energy onto the child creating a 'snowball effect' of anxiety passing between adults to child, becoming a never-ending cycle.
- Children are extremely intuitive and are like sponges. They feel everything, but it is not part of the developmental guidance in our system to be taught the understanding of intuitive intelligence. Intuition governs the child's senses and faculties until the *normal* world and training from the establishment kicks in and overrules it.
- A lack of self-awareness results from this system which throws kids into a cookie-cutter existence that doesn't support the essence of who each child is as an individual.

I'd like to close this chapter by saying it is important to note that because a child appears to be anxious, angry, upset and/or misbehaving does not mean the child is disordered. It is not necessarily the case that a real illness is involved. It is always important to rule out the possibility that children's behavior or symptoms of anxiety could be in response to a trigger or stressor in the child's environment. As adults, our best practice would be to help our child by looking for solutions beyond merely treating the 'symptoms' (the stress of negative behavior) and endeavor to discover the environmental 'trigger' which is causing the child's symptoms of negative behavior and anxiety in the first place.

Chapter 3

Yoga & Mindfulness, and the Importance of Effective Communication

"A child seldom needs a good talking to as a good listening to" – Robert Brault

YOGA IS A discipline which includes breath control, meditation, and the practice of bodily postures to enhance well-being, health and relaxation. Yoga is simple to learn and easy to incorporate into any busy schedule. The techniques learnt in yoga can be applied at any time of the day, almost anywhere and do not require any special clothing or expensive equipment or tools. In fact yoga can be so simple that even very young children can learn the techniques on their own and can be taught to practice them during times when they feel stressed, overwhelmed or insecure and need to feel calm and safe.

Yoga for children requires a very different approach to teaching that yoga for adults because children and adults are both very different; however there is nothing wrong with you as an adult using the techniques and strategies outlined in this book to help yourself too! I do!

The key to success with the yoga for kids is that it needs to become a discipline, which means regular practice and during times when the child is calm and relaxed, that way he will not resist the work. The second thing is try to pick a time of the day after bath or before bed and practice it at the exact same time habitually because the mind will accept it more readily.

One of the fundamental aspects I like to focus on in therapeutic yoga for children is effective communication through self-awareness, self-expression and active listening during our yoga class activities and exercises. Effective communication begins with knowing yourself well and understanding how you are feeling.

When children learn to become self-aware through the practice of yoga and mindfulness they become able to effectively express their thoughts, feelings and needs with both their peers and the adults around them.

Effective communication is the function of the throat chakra centre of energy located in the throat. Effective communication is not just about being able to verbally communicate your personal needs and opinions, it is equally about being able to listen to other people's truths without feeling threatened, or reacting from a place of fear or defensiveness.

Teaching children how to communicate effectively through the practice of yoga and mindfulness is a fantastic way for children to learn about how they relate and interact with others early in their lives. These skills help children develop healthy positive attitudes toward relationships as youngsters, and become the foundation of healthy relationships with others as they grow into their teens and adulthood.

Why effective communication is important for children in their formative years:

- Children become less likely to be the target of an abusive relationship later in life.
- Children will grow up feeling a sense of purpose.
- Children will grow up feeling empowered to make positive life choices.
- and live a more fulfilled life.
- There will be less instances of mood/behavioral disorders, anxiety and depression, and less need for psychiatric drugs both during childhood and adulthood.

Yoga and mindfulness exercises for children are proving to be effective in terms of helping children with their performance at school too. I have been fortunate to have had the opportunity to teach yoga and mindfulness in our local elementary school both as part of the regular curriculum, and in the after school program. The children I teach are between the ages of four and ten.

It has been reported from the teachers that the practice of yoga and mindfulness is reflecting in the children's day-to-day life at school in positive ways. For example: their adaptation to their schoolwork; more relaxed relationships with peers; and their increased ability to communicate with their teachers.

The exercises that I have shared with the school children during our lessons are outlined in the later chapters of this book. The exercises shared here are the ones which I feel are best suited to work with the central theme and intention of this book, to enhance simplicity and ease.

Chapter 4

Creating Space for Children

"You may give them your love but not your thoughts.
For they have their own thoughts.
You may house their bodies but not their souls,
For their souls dwell in the house of tomorrow,
which you cannot visit, not even in your dreams.
You may strive to be like them, but seek not to make them
like you.
For life goes not backward nor tarries with yesterday."
– Kahlil Gibran, On Children

CREATING SPACE FOR your child to thrive and grow within is as much about giving him mental and emotional space as it is physical.

As an adult, if you are unhappy with your childhood and have not yet come to terms with your own unfulfilled dreams, failures and disappointments, it is not uncommon to look to your children as an opportunity to have a second chance to make up for what was lost during your youth. Living through your child, by expecting her to live out your own dreams, goals and accomplishments is an act of unconscious emotional abuse, even when in your heart you are convinced you are doing something to help your child succeed.

As parents, teachers, guardians or caregivers is it our responsibility to create a safe space within which our children can become who they really are. As I mentioned before space is more than physical, it is mental and emotional too. Although all kinds of space are important to encourage a child's development, the space I am specifically referring to in this chapter is the space within which provides the ability for children to express themselves freely and safely with acceptance as opposed to pushing, forcing, pressure or judgment.

How do I know if I giving my child space? The first element of being able to step into a place where you can create space for your child is by asking yourself these questions:

- Am I able to step back and focus on my child's well-being first?
- Is my approach to parenting about me or my child?
- Do I feel emotionally intelligent as an adult?
- Do I feel a sense of wellness within myself?
- Do I know who I really am?
- Do I feel fulfilled enough within myself to stop living through my child?
- Can I let go of expectations of who I think my child ought to be?

As parents, it is not our job to force our children to become who we think they should be. * It is our job to create the space within which they can become who they really are. We can do this by removing our own emotional baggage from the things we wish we had done or accomplished, and then entertaining inauthentic expectations and projecting them onto our children.

Projecting expectations of who you wish you had become, or using your child to fulfill a stand you would like in your life is unfair and will lead to a life for your child which is based upon inauthentic expectations. In short, his life will be a lie.

If a child's inherited beliefs of who he is, is based on a set of criteria that do not fit, and are not in alignment with who he really is, he will grow up to have a fragmented view of himself.

Many adults try to impose their own unrealized dreams and ideals onto their children. Children are themselves, they are not you! It is not fair to impose an inauthentic life upon your children. It will put them under unnecessary pressure and confusion that does not belong to them.

Any form of pressure upon a child, or an adult for that matter creates a feeling of discomfort and as a result will cause resistance. When a child becomes resistant to a situation in his life he will try to communicate it. As we discussed in chapter two, when a child is communicating with adults who are not listening or understanding what he is saying, he will likely turn to negative or defiant behavior to make his statement. Resistance creates more resistance and this will fuel the fire for stress and anxiety to grow between the parent and child. So to resolve this, try to sit back and hear what your child is trying to tell you. If he does not want to be or do the things you are trying to force him to (such as multiple dance classes, piano lessons, soccer practice, tennis and the like), listen and ask him what is it *he would like to do*. If he doesn't know yet, then step back and allow him to have space away from all the other pressures to take a breath and find out on his own.

Our children are not our trophies, they are people. I see so many parents of young children these days enrolling their children into a multitude of different activities. Getting dragged to school - a chore for many children -day after day, and then taken to activities after school as well can become confusing especially if these activities are ones that *you* have chosen. To become a master at anything you have to focus on that one thing and give it your all until you have mastered it. Scattering energies and attention between a cornucopia of things is confusing, exhausting and does not allow you to really become a master of anything so in the end your efforts are likely to be redundant. I understand that many adults will argue that how can a child know what they like unless they 'try out everything.' My answer to that is: how will they ever think about liking anything when they are so confused between so many options? The other answer is that when a child has space to reflect upon what she wants to do and what she is interested in, she will let you know.

My experience with my own son Robbie is a perfect example of this. Robbie expressed interest in soccer from a very early age and so we signed him up for soccer camp at age four. His coaches recognized that he was showing above average skills in the sport so that is the sport he committed to and has loved ever since. Did I want him to be a soccer player? Not really! Personally, when I saw him the first moment he was born, I saw his long fingers and thought 'I hope he becomes a pianist.' I signed him up for music for tots when he was only months old and it was fun. However, as he grew older I noticed he was not showing much of an interest in it. He later started showing resistance which manifested as a great deal of whining, crying fussing and refusing to go and as a result, I listened to him and removed him from music and felt sad about it for a while.

Upon reflection much later, I realized becoming a musician was my own unrealized dream that I was projecting on my son. I had studied music since I was four. I learned to play violin from the age of eight and also played tenor recorder in a very successful school recorder group. I studied for music exams, played in multiple orchestras, competed in music competitions and festivals and continued to do so till I had to stop due to life circumstances that were not of my choice at age 16.

Since then my heart has been heavy because I was not able to pursue my passion for music. A huge part of my life and who I was seemed to just vanish when I stopped music. I tried to continue with music by buying a violin, taking lessons and even joined an orchestra later when I reached my 30's but by this time it was too late as I was far too busy with my children and work to be able to pursue it at the level I dreamed of.

I worked on accepting all of this and let it all go. As a mother I am glad I was able to realize that it is not fair to project my unrealized dreams on to my own child sooner rather than later. I realized my son is not me; he is himself and has other goals and aspirations to accomplish in his life; he is not here to live out mine and we have never looked back; so I did not mention courses, lessons or camps until my children asked me. My son is still a soccer star and continues to do excellently in soccer and wants to play professionally. My daughter took her time but has started tennis lessons this year and also expressed interest in "winning a trophy" I am proud of them not because they want to excel and win over others, I am proud because my children have taken the time to choose their own interests and because of that every effort they make to succeed will be fired by the fuel of their own inner longing and inspiration, not with the fear-based feeling of having to succeed to please me or anyone else.

What drives a child's motivation is what defines whether they will be successful in the true sense of what it means to be successful in life. One of the greatest lessons I learnt during my early

15

teens is that success is happiness, and happiness is your success. Regardless of what you are doing if you are happy, truly happy you are successful. You are not successful if you are miserable and unfulfilled even if you are a champion at what you are doing. If you dislike it and are doing it to please others, you are yet to find your true success.

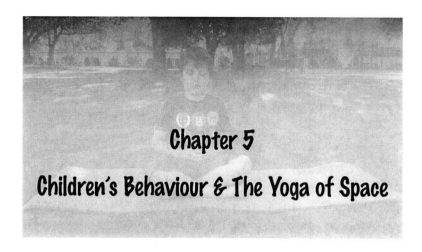

Chapter 5

Children's Behaviour & The Yoga of Space

"Your children are not your children. They are the sons and daughters of Life's longing for itself." - Kahlil Gibran

AT THIS PART of the book, I'd like to delve more deeply into the discussion of the yoga system which is the system upon which is the basis of my holistic health care and therapeutic work with others, and is also the basis for all the mindfulness techniques I will offer in the second half of the book.

The Yoga system is an ancient art and science which was practiced and perfected in India thousands of years ago. The foundations of yogic philosophy were written down in Patanjali's *The Yoga Sutra* in approximately 200 AD. The Yoga Sutra describes the workings of the mind and outlines an eight-fold path to follow for controlling its restlessness so as to enjoy a deep sense of inner peace and bliss.

The practice of yoga is dedicated to creating union between body, mind and spirit. Through the physical body and the breath, the objective of yoga is to assist the yogi to awaken to a deeper sense of himself as an individual, and to the awareness that he is connected to the whole of creation. Yoga teaches you about finding balance and living moderately in order to live peacefully, healthily and harmoniously with yourself, those around you, and your environment.

The Path of Yoga

The eight-fold path of the Yoga Sutra provides a structured framework for practicing yoga. No aspect of the eight-fold path is more relevant or important than another. All aspects of the path are equally as significant. When you practice each part holistically it eventually leads to an experience of profound peace and wholeness.

Here is a brief listing of the steps outlined on the eight-fold path of yoga:

1. Yama : Morals
2. Niyama : Personal observances
3. Asanas : Postures
4. Pranayama : Breathing exercises
5. Pratyahara : Withdrawal of the mind from the senses
6. Dharana : Concentration
7. Dhyana : Meditation
8. Samadhi : Divine Union

The first two steps on the yoga path describe the fundamental ethical principles called *yamas* and *niyamas*. Yamas and niyamas are the ideals about how we should deal with people around us, our environment and our ideal attitude toward ourselves. Both are mainly concerned with how we use our energy in our inner and outer worlds. Our attitude toward things and people outside ourselves is yama, and how we relate to ourselves inwardly is niyama.

Niyama means *rules* or *laws*. These are the rules prescribed for personal observance. Like the yamas, the five niyamas are not exercises or actions to be simply studied; they must be put into practice in order to be experienced. They represent more than just an attitude, and are guidelines to follow to achieve a life lived soulfully.

For the sake of this chapter's discussion we will concern ourselves with the first observance from the niyamas which is *saucha* meaning *purity* and *cleanliness*. Sauca has both an inner and an outer aspect. Outer cleanliness simply means keeping ourselves clean. Inner cleanliness has to do with the healthy functioning of our body and with the clarity of our mind. Sauca and living purely, involves maintaining a level cleanliness in body, mind, and our environment so that we can experience ourselves, and enjoy our life experience at a higher level.

The Yoga of Space

If the word Yoga means *to yoke*, to bring body, mind and spirit together as one and to connect with the creative energy of nature, then why are space and the outer environment so important on a path which encourages us to be so focused inwardly?

Like human beings, physical objects also consist of energy that is vibrating at a lower vibrational frequency. The rate at which the energy of an object vibrates does not necessarily make it bad or negative; however, when you have too many objects around you in a disorganized fashion it creates clutter, which becomes a negative.

The energy of the physical environment and other people's energies that exist in physical space are an important factor in affecting how children feel and behave. Because children are so sensitive and young, they are only just developing a sense of who they are, and so it can be hard for them to distinguish what is their energy, and what is not. It can be confusing because they might feel overwhelmed, and even afraid due to the influence of the physical space they are in yet not really know why they feel the way they do because the energy of space is not something that we typically educate our children, or even ourselves as adults about.

'Clutter' is a word which is typically used to describe the state of a room which is in disarray and filled with too many objects and 'stuff'. The effect of clutter can be explained as a mass of stuff creating a state of disorganization. Physical objects have energetic vibrations and produce energetic frequencies which affect our environment and its mood in the same way as being around a happy or a grumpy person affects the energy of a room. So in essence, clutter creates a congestion of different energetic vibrations coinciding with each other at once.

A cluttered environment causes confusion in the mind and in our own energies. It creates a sense of inner disarray. When our energies are 'scattered' in this way it becomes impossible to focus and feel centered. Our creativity slows down, or comes to a halt as a result and we cannot come into contact with the deepest and most peaceful part of ourselves while surrounded by clutter. Clarity and cleanliness of space leads to clarity of mind which in turn leads us to experiencing a deeper sense of peace and happiness.

If you have a child who appears to be anxious, take a good look at the environment the child is living in. How tidy is your home?

How much 'stuff' is lying around? Is it organized? Do you leave dirty laundry, dishes and other objects lying around? How is the child's bedroom looking? Is it packed to the brim with toys so much so that you cannot see any space on the floor? Is the bed made? Are his clothes organized so that he can choose his clothes easily in the morning? What is the color scheme like? Is his room decorated with calming and relaxing colors, or are the colors over-stimulating and too energetic?

These seem like basic aspects to consider when figuring out what potential triggers for your child's mood and behavior could be, and funnily enough they are. This is what is so amazing about working with the energy of space to alter how your child feels and behaves as a result. It really is as simple as tidying up.

Looking for answers to trackmental and emotional challenges in children can be daunting and look like a struggle; however, it doesn't always have to be. I am also NOT claiming that tidying up your space is the cure to any and all of your child's mental or emotional challenges, but it is definitely a great place to start diffusing the situation into a clearer and calmer scenario.

Cleaning up your space will not only benefit your child's state of being/feeling, it will also help yours as a parent. You too will feel calmer and more focused with a sense of clarity on how to handle things more effectively and with conviction if you are in a clean and tidy environment.

Considering my own young children, I can tell you from experience that when my children's room is in disarray their attitudes are different, their energy levels are different, the way they interact changes and the way they communicate with each other becomes strained, and of course all in a negative way. I always encourage them to tidy their room and then they will feel more relaxed and calm being where they are.

Teaching your children to maintain an environment of tidiness and cleanliness comes first by setting the example, and then it is from taking responsibility. Children love having a 'job' so entrust them with the 'super important job' of being in charge of cleaning their own space. Children thrive when they are given the space to exercise responsibility. It also gives their confidence and self-esteem a real boost when they see the amazing results of their hard work tidying up. Don't forget to give them plenty of praise for their efforts too. It will not make them lazy or passive when you congratulate them. On the contrary, it will make them more eager to take responsibility for their room in future.

To close this chapter I'd like to summarize that a tidy and clean room not only will increase both your child's and your own peace of mind as you both feel more relaxed, grounded and centered. It will also give the child more space in which to play, create, reflect and relax more effectively, and this sets the stage for some great mindfulness practice. It really is as simple as that!

Chapter 6

Yoga for Anxious Children

ANXIETY IS A common experience in our world today. It is not just children, but adults who experience anxiety too. Our world can create feelings of uncertainty for anyone. However, children's lack of understanding about the world around them, their small bodies, and lack of control in situations can make their anxiety feel much worse.

Unlike adults, as we have discussed in the previous chapters, often children do not have the emotional maturity, understanding or vocabulary to verbally communicate their anxious feelings or emotions. Children can express their anxious feelings in a variety of different ways such as behaving differently, acting up, appearing withdrawn, crying, bed-wetting, being picky with foods and generally just being what we would describe as 'difficult', but in a more than typical and dramatic way.

Having a child who is anxious can be an extremely emotionally trying experience for you. It is a challenge, and as much as you would like to do anything to help calm the child's emotions, you probably have no idea where to start.

It is always important to remember that children are not fully developed when it comes to understanding, recognizing and managing emotional responses. Learning when we need to, and how to comfort ourselves is something that we develop as we grow. Parenting an anxious child can be tough, however it is not impossible. It is as easy as knowing a few easy ways to calm your child, then teach her how to calm herself (referring to my daughter).

Yoga can help both you and your anxious child, and later chapters of this book will offer practical techniques in yoga to help your child manage anxiety. Although you can practice with your child, it is important to remember that the yoga that adults practice is not exactly the same as yoga for kids. If you would like to try using yoga to help manage your child's anxiety, you will need to follow a few modifications that make the yoga practice more effective. Yoga for kids has to make exercise, breathing and visualization fun. If it seems like a chore, children will likely lose interest and won't want to take part for long.

Teaching yoga to children experiencing anxiety gives them the opportunity to:

- Learn that yoga can help them to combat their anxious feelings through the practice of movement and breathing.
- Learn that meditation and calming visualization techniques can help quieten and calm their mind and train them to be able to choose their thoughts.
- Learn to listen to calming and relaxing music as it is a tool which can influence how they feel.

Regular yoga practice is crucial. It is better to commit to a ten minute session each day, rather than one long session once a week. Consistency is key in yoga as it is a discipline of which the techniques learnt soon become new behaviors and a way of life.

It is crucial to focus on introducing yoga therapies into your child's routine during relaxed and calm moments. If you wait until your child is having a 'dramatic moment' then the chances are it will be rejected. The yoga needs to become a habit, a way of life and something that is normal for your child to do. This is when the child will finally become empowered enough to recognize how he is feeling, and use the exercises he has learnt in yoga to soothe himself without too much drama or resistance occurring.

You will see the benefits of yoga build slowly after days, weeks and months of practice. You will need to find ways of making yoga more of a challenge as time goes on. Children tend to get sidetracked, bored or discouraged easily if an activity is not stimulating enough to keep them engaged. Yoga for kids also has to be fun, not a chore that they may resist. Yoga will not be helpful if the child feels he is being forced into participating.

You can keep yoga stimulating and interesting by:

- Creating fun names for postures.
- Inventing new postures based on things your child loves.
- Make a mini yoga sequence out of a story your child enjoys.
- Encourage siblings to join in too.
- Make it a team effort as you help guide your child through postures.
- Rewarding children for their participation.
- Use colors for themes and visualizations during exercises.

Yoga practice typically consists of gentle, slow body movements and breathing with focused attention and concentration. The bodily movements involved in yoga play a key role in addressing the symptoms of anxiety. Yoga's rhythmic and intentional approach to breathing and movement provides an excellent way for anxious children to learn strong coping skills.

All in all, yoga can help children to feel calmer inside, become more focused mentally and learn how to recognize, adapt to and manage fear and uncomfortable feelings instead of panicking. It is a complete mind and body system to enhance wellness on every level - mind body and spirit - and can be incorporated into your child's routine in many simple, creative ways.

Chapter 7

Knowing the Difference Between Tension & Relaxation

AS ADULTS MANY of us live in a chronic state of muscular tension and anxiety which gets worse when we face times of increased stress. But what about children? Children are under considerable stress too as they face greater demands at school. Our children are under pressure in overcrowded, under-funded, split-grade class rooms immersed within a 'cookie cutter' curriculum of lessons they are forced to learn, whether they like it or not, and it affects them in ways which can be detrimental to their mental health and well-being.

One of the fundamental lessons in Yoga, or any other holistically based therapy, is that whenever you experience anxiety, stress or fear in your mind and emotions, it is eventually expressed in your physical body. You may not even realize that your muscles are tense all the time as it has probably become normal for you to feel that way. Think about what you do when you're stressed. Do you tense your shoulders, frown, clench your jaw, or hold your breath?

What do children do when they are stressed? As children, it is a bit harder to handle stress than it is for adults because, as we have discussed they have neither the emotional intelligence, nor the vocabulary we do to be able to properly understand and express how they are feeling. Fortunately, teaching emotional intelligence and self-awareness is something that we are seeing increasingly as a part of the school curriculum.

When children feel anxious or afraid then they will act out on it, typically through withdrawal, or through negative behaviors as this is effective to them in terms of getting attention from adults. This was discussed early on in this book, and I touch upon it several times as I believe chronic stress and anxiety it is at the root of many behavioral issues we are facing with our children these days.

The common eventuality during a scenarios of misbehavior is that the child is assumed to have either a learning, or some disorder and as a result ends up in either learning support with a damaged self-esteem, or in a psychiatrist's office facing a diagnosis of psychiatric illness, often leading to a prescription of mind-altering drugs. This is the unfortunate reality many of our children are facing these days due to the pressures of our system.

Helping your child to develop emotional intelligence and self-awareness need not be rocket science, and that is where the beauty of yoga enters the equation. Later in the book we will explore a series of yoga exercises designed to teach children to find their muscles, squeeze them tight and then relax them. This allows them to learn how to recognize when their bodies are tense, and when they are relaxed. It also helps the child to instantly relax and creates a sense of well-being as energy and blood circulation is enhanced with this practice. Children also find this exercise fun as it teaches them about their anatomy!

Becoming mindfully aware of the difference between tension and relaxation helps to create an internal physical alarm which will help children to become aware of when they are starting to feel anxious. Teaching your children self-awareness, and encouraging them to express how he or she is feeling is the first step toward helping boost your child's mental health.

Although we will explore yoga exercises in depth later in the book, you can begin practicing right away with this simple exercise if you feel you need to begin practice with your child right away. The key is to start practicing this exercise during times when your child is already relaxed so that when he does feel anxious, he accepts the exercise easily.

To begin, find a quiet place that is free of distractions. Ask your child to either lie down or sit comfortably in a chair. As you work through this exercise, ask your child to squeeze different muscles in different parts of his body as hard as he can for a few seconds, and then release quickly so that he can begin to learn about how his body experiences and expresses tightness and tension. If he has difficulty at first, you can help him by squeezing the different body parts lightly to introduce the idea of feeling the difference between a tense foot and a relaxed foot, for example, then when he is ready you can guide him through the sequence all the way up the body to the face.

In some cases children might grow restless, especially when they are new to these types of practices so have patience and go at the child's pace. The more often you practice the exercise with your child, the more accustomed to the exercise he will become and you can eventually work through the whole sequence.

See Chapter 14's *Five Minutes to Meditate* exercise for the more in-depth look at the exercise *Lemon Face Meditation* to help your child recognize and release anxiety and tension in his body.

Chapter 8
ADHD - Beyond the Diagnosis

*"The children who need love the most will always ask for
it in the most unloving ways"* — *Russell Barkley*

I LIKE TO call ADHD our 'New Age dis-ease'. Contrary to what
some controversial scientific research tells us about the cause
of ADHD, I believe that ADHD is a symptomatic response
associated with the pressure of living during such demanding
times.

As the world gets faster and crazier, the symptoms that define
ADHD become prevalent and more prominent. Approximately
six million children in N. America alone have been diagnosed
with an attention deficit disorderand prescribed with psycho-
stimulant drugs, such as 'Methylphenidate', otherwise known
by its brand name 'Ritalin', as the primary method of treatment.

The question to ask is: What is ADHD really? Why are so many
children being diagnosed with it these days, and what could be
the real cause of it? Also, how much do we really know about
the effects of stimulant drugs on our children? How will taking

these drugs affect children's lives physiologically, psychologically, emotionally and socially as they grow up?

Asking these questions are what led me to research yoga as an alternative natural holistic strategy for dealing with the symptoms associated with ADHD in children when I was studying for my doctorate in metaphysical science.

Attention Deficit Disorder, or ADHD, is said to manifest in early childhood as a behavioral disorder which is defined as a deficiency in age-appropriate attention, impulse control and the inability to follow directions and structured activities.

Behaviors associated with the ADHD diagnosis include:

- Hyperactivity.
- Speaking or acting before one thinks.
- Difficulty in following instructions.
- Poor organizational skills.
- Restlessness.
- Impatience.
- Forgetfulness.
- Low self-esteem.
- Poor social skills.

Children displaying the symptoms that are associated with the ADHD diagnosis find it difficult to slow down, even when they want to. These children are often so hurried that they seem clumsy and uncoordinated which can often lead to them hurting themselves or others. As well, children diagnosed with ADHD generally do not perform well in school, though most of them test at average or above average intelligence.

There are many possible factors contributing to this alleged behavioral disorder, and the fact that so many children are being diagnosed with ADHD. For example:

- TV violence.
- Overstimulation from video games/TV.
- Lack of physical exercise.
- Poor nutrition.
- Parental prenatal drug use.
- Sensory overload.
- Pollution.
- Overcrowding.
- Breakdown of the family structure.

Yoga is an effective system for helping children and their families to deal with the behaviors associated with ADHD on a physical level through the practice of postures or 'asana' in a non-competitive way. This can help enhance a child's sense of body awareness, self-control, patience and respect for other people's physical space. The fact that Yoga is typically practiced on a mat introduces the concept of personal space, and teaches a child that there are boundaries between her physical space to move within, and that of other people around her.

On a deeper level, meditation practice can help bring you beyond the surface of the behavioral issues that children are experiencing to reveal what lies at the root of the challenges, to understand them and deal with them. Meditation will also help the child to connect with his inner essence, his Spirit and his Soul. When he becomes more aware of whom he is on a deeper level, he will be more able to express this to his mother and father, and teacher.

Another exercise children respond particularly well to is guided visualization with imagery. It helps children to relax and calm down as their inner creativity is invoked and stimulated through use of their imagination. This yoga technique opens children's minds as they are allowed to run free in their own mental landscape. This type of mental freedom helps them to build confidence in their own creative abilities, and as a result leads to higher self-esteem and a deeper level of trust.

The spiritual aspect of Yoga helps ground practitioners in their own silence and inner awareness, something that is becoming increasingly difficult to experience in our busy pace of life today. Yoga also teaches us about personal responsibility and that all our actions and choices create the circumstances and experiences that we encounter in our life.

As well, the practice of partner Yoga between the parent and child can help build trust and mutual respect for each other as individual people, as well as being part of the parent/child connection. Yoga in this sense can help rebuild, strengthen and solidify relationships within families on many levels in unique, fun and interesting ways.

Similar to what we discussed earlier in the chapter in *Yoga for Children with Anxiety*, practicing Yoga gives children experiencing symptoms associated with ADHD the opportunity to:

- Learn that movement can actually combat feelings of restlessness.
- Practice in a safe, non-judgmental environment.
- Learn how to control, and use their breath to influence how they feel.
- Learn that meditation can help them to calm their mind and choose their thoughts.

- Build self-esteem and confidence by improving their yoga skills.
- Feel great about their bodies as they grow in strength, flexibility and balance.
- Feel like members of a community if they are in a kid's yoga class.
- Practice calming visualization techniques.
- Understand how relaxing music can influence their energy levels.
- Learn about respect for their body, and others because the practice of yoga is normally confined to your own mat space.

Again, regular yoga practice is crucial. As mentioned before in the chapter on yoga for anxious children, and especially for children diagnosed with ADHD, it is more effective to commit to short, five minute sessions each day that you can gradually build upon, rather than one long session once a week. This way your child will feel a sense of encouragement with what has been accomplished in his yoga practice, as oppose to forcing the child into a longer session that could potentially create a sense of boredom and resistance. Consistency is key in yoga, not the length of time you practice. It is a discipline where the techniques learnt soon express themselves as new behaviors and a new 'normal' way of life.

There are a multitude of postures and yoga games kids can try; however I like 'Deep Belly Breathing', 'Downward Facing Dog' and 'Tree Pose' for combating behaviors associated with ADHD. These exercises are quick and easy to use any time. See the section 'Five Minutes to Move' for an outline of effective yoga poses that can help you and your child manage the symptoms associated with ADHD.

Yoga provides a complete system above all others which, if practiced both physically and spiritually, can provide the basis for a way of life incorporating physical, emotional and spiritual understanding and well-being in a natural, healthy and holistic way.

Regardless of how spooky their state-of-mind diagnosis or creepy the alphabet labels, children are never too young to begin learning about simple personal responsibility. Understanding responsibility will help them to understand that their behavior influences what happens to them every day. Children feel empowered in knowing that they have a choice in terms of how they behave and interact with others and their environment. A sense of personal responsibility along with a feeling of empowerment to choose will no doubt lead to better behavior from a calmer and more confident child.

When parents/teachers are able to acknowledge, accept and relate to who their child really is beyond the ADHD diagnosis, and what that child is trying to express through actions and behaviors then the child will no longer be misunderstood and viewed as being dysfunctional. This is very important for the child's sense of self-worth and success in future, and our future depends on us raising a generation of healthy, confident, creative-empowered children.

Chapter 9

The Rise of Technology & how it affects our Children

TECHNOLOGY HAS BECOME an influential force in our world so much so that it has influenced the speed at which we are able to communicate, access information and quickly connect with other people on the other side of the globe in within seconds.

Internet, social media, email, text messaging and interactive video games have made communication and entertainment, simpler, quicker and a whole lot better. However, what effect does this have on us as we become more and more accustomed to having everything so fast, and at the touch of a button?

In an already fast world I have started to notice that as it becomes easier to obtain the information we need so quickly, people are becoming less and less tolerant of waiting and as a result that translates into feelings of impatience, stress, frustration and even anger when people do not get what they want as quickly as they'd like to.

I have witnessed in stores, airports and in the bank people literally flying into a rage of frustration or impatience because they cannot simply walk in and have what they want, when they want it and at the drop of a hat. People are becoming less and less tolerant of having to wait to be attended to and get things done and in my opinion this is because of the rise of technology which makes things so easy for us that we expect the whole world to run faster.

Technology seems to have stepped in and is taking over our world so much so that relationships are being affected as people spend less and less time sitting together, connecting as people in real life and the way to mingle these days is virtually on social media. The personal connection is fading out and what kind of an example is this setting for our children? How does technology affect our children and how they relate to the world and people around them are important questions I have been pondering lately.

Children are already being exposed to cell phones, computerized phones, watches and game consoles from a very young age. On many occasions when we have went out to dinner, or out shopping for example, we have seen children set up with laptops, phones with video games and little hand-held game consoles just to keep them entertained and quiet while out and about. And while, of course, I understand why parents would do this to keep the child busy and to avoid distraction, I wonder why choose a fantasy (and usually violent) mind-numbing, video game to entertain the child as opposed to a book or some art activities to stimulate the child's mind and creativity?

It concerns me a great deal to see so many children these days already hooked on video games. The affect these games have on children are not positive and although many would argue that the games help promote team work, thinking, intellectual abilities and strategic skills that are required to win the game, I, on the other hand, argue that while these might seem like benefits, there are a great deal of negatives which far outweigh the benefits of letting your child play a video game.

The first things I like to discuss is that by allowing children to play video games too much we are conditioning them to become the way we are becoming as adults when it comes to dealing with the real world in real time. Everything is slower and less stimulating in the real world than it is in a video game so children can begin to develop feelings of frustration and dissatisfaction with the pace of the real world.

When children play video games that involve shooting, killing and winning, what happens is that the reward centers in the brain are stimulated and release the neurotransmitter dopamine. Dopamine is associated with the 'pleasure system' of the brain, providing feelings of enjoyment and the motivation to do, or continue to do, certain activities which make us feel good. Dopamine is released by rewarding experiences such as eating and drinking. In children, dopamine is released during the times of heightened pleasure and stimulation of playing their video games, meaning that as more and more game-playing produces more and more reward, the brain becomes accustomed to having such a sense of reward from the game that the child needs more and more stimulus and all other activities which do not produce the same level of stimuli or excitement become boring.

This really begins to affect the child on many levels from socially to educationally because if the child is not receiving the same level of reward or stimulation as he is used to from the increased use of video games, he will become bored with friends, school, and any other activities that do not involve playing video games.

The aspect of the this which really concerns me is that in one hand we allow our children to have such a great deal of exposure to technology and allow them to grow accustomed to having a great deal of stimulation from the games without really knowing how it affects them. Then we send them off into the real world at school, for example, where they are forced to sit in a room all day, learn lessons, do exercises and work which is nowhere near as exciting as the video game they played for hours the night before and expect them to adjust. Next thing you know is that the teacher is calling home wanting to meet with the parent because it is such a concern that the child is not listening, fidgeting, day-dreaming and not paying attention and is displaying behaviors associated with the ADHD diagnosis.

We are setting our children up for failure this way and we cannot expect them at such a young age to be able to adapt so readily to such a change in pace from a video game to a classroom.

We really need to limit the time children spend with technology and gaming devices. Instead of letting a TV or a computer entertain or take care of them when you are busy or out and about, give them a book or a drawing pad to start stimulating their creativity and imagination. Let them get bored. There is nothing wrong with it. During a period of boredom is when we become most innovative and great ideas have the space to come to life. Boredom is not always a bad thing, it can also be inspiring. Let your child be bored and give him a chance to discover his own creative genius and allow him the space to express it. Keep the crayons and sketch book handy! You will not regret it!

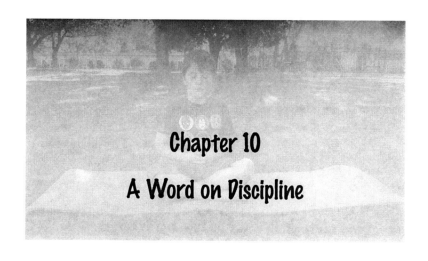

Chapter 10

A Word on Discipline

"If we don't shape our kids, they will be shaped by outside forces that don't care what shape our kids are in." - Dr. Louise Hart

I WANTED TO touch on the subject of discipline briefly because the idea of disciplining your child is becoming quite a controversial matter in this day and age. Before we delve into the discussion, let's look at what discipline means. According to Google's dictionary the word *'discipline'* is defined as *'the practice of training people to obey rules or a code of behavior, using punishment to correct disobedience.'* Interestingly here is one of the examples they have listed where *'discipline'* appears as a noun in a sentence *'many parents have been afraid to discipline their children'*.

This is an interesting lead into this chapter to discuss discipline. These days people are afraid to discipline their children and that disciplining your child in many cases is considered as child abuse. On the contrary: I think that NOT disciplining your child is harmful to children. It all depends on how you define discipline and how you do it.

Children these days are being born into our world with heightened intuition, stronger spirits and sharper minds. They are extremely intelligent individuals who I believe have been born into our world at this time to make great changes by reshaping the system we live in. While children cannot create change by conforming or simply 'fitting-in', they also cannot create change by becoming unruly, disrespectful and rude for these are not the behaviors that will later inspire them to become the leaders, thought provokers and game-changers that will lift the world and human consciousness to the next level. Quite the contrary: it is the negative behaviors that will turn our children into rebels and, God forbid, criminals. I have sat back and watched parents allow their children to be disrespectful to them in public, or to teachers at the school and in class; or in the park. Sometimes, I am wondering who the parent is and who the child is in the relationship. Who on earth is the leader: the child or the adult?

Strong children need a strong leader to guide them, not someone whose main motivation is to avoid upsetting them. Really strong children who act out in ways that are rebellious and defiant are crying out for a strong leader, not an adult who is terrified to offend the child. It is time to do some inner work, step up to the plate and into the leadership mode and trust me, in the end these children will respect you more.

Discipline is not about laying down a heavy hand on your child. Au contraire! It is about having the self-control, self-confidence, self-assuredness and the courage to step up and let the child know what is right and wrong, or appropriate or inappropriate behavior regardless of how he may feel about being corrected; and this means he may not always like you, and it may not always be a pleasant conversation.

Children are extremely intuitive and if you are operating from a place of fear, guilt, self-doubt or lack of self-confidence, they will sense this and use that to step up and take the reins in the relationship.

In my experience from the years of being a mother of two and a caregiver and teacher of children, I have realized that children have this amazing gift of being able to bring some of your weaknesses to the surface.For example, they are experts in trying your patience! They make you acknowledge it and hopefully work toward transforming it into an amazing opportunity to change, grow and evolve as a result. This is what I have learnt and has this learning has made me a stronger leader and a better mother.

All the children I have encountered one way or another have inspired me to look into my worst character traits, my knee-jerk reactions and foolish habits on a daily basis. They force me to become aware of them, acknowledge them and work toward changing them in any way I can so I can better guide the little people I deal with. From the very moment I discovered I was pregnant, right through tochildbirth and into motherhood, my own children have also made me face my fears and walk through them, and because of them I feel I have been successful in the way I deal with, and teach children.

Children have taught me patience, consideration, selflessness, sacrifice, commitment, consideration, co-operation, responsibility, and most of all unconditional love. Unconditional love means not just letting them run riot doing whatever they want, whenever they please. It means having the strength to step up and let them know that their behavior is unacceptable, and explaining why so that they discover that you are not damaging them in any way by showing them a better path. Eventually with time and observation, you will see that all along the little people have been starving for proper guidance from an adult who is not afraid and unsure. Children pick up on feelings of uncertainty, it makes them feel insecure and when children are insecure, they act up. As a result you can see that a lack of proper discipline can escalate children's negative behavior, and increasingly worsen the situation.

The children today are not here with boundless energy because they are mentally diseased and disordered. They are here with vibrant, elevated and very advanced energies to help challenge us, and bring out the best and worst in us so we can learn to embrace the lighter side of our nature, within which vibrates love, compassion and selflessness. When we connect with that part of ourselves, we are connecting to our higher nature and when that energy permeates who we are and our nature, then the process of evolution into higher states of being begins, and the energetic vibration of our entire planet will evolve too as a result.

At this point in our worldly progression, the Universe is urging us to change, to grow and to move forth with the evolutionary tides. However, while we remain caught up living in states of fear, greed, hate, blame, rage and judgment, we can never move forward, and will stagnate in our growth.

As I said before, the children that we are seeing in our society today are not different because they are diseased or dysfunctional children. They are different yes, but because they are here to help our world to transition into the next stage of our growth, evolution and conscious awareness of our essence and higher purpose here in this world. These 'challenged' children have opted to come here at this point in time to serve us, and the Universe by assisting in the cycle of evolutionary progression.

Many of these children are very advanced and wise souls who have no karmic obligation of their own that requires them to enter into the physical world at this point of their karmic progression. Ultimately, they are motivated by their deep sense of love, compassion and unconditional love which vibrates deep within them as their true nature. I believe they came here knowing, andanticipating the difficult conditions they may face as children, because they have opted to come and express themselves in ways which will defy the system we have become accustomed to living in for so long, to shake it up and hopefully, change it. They must defy the system because it is a system that no longer serves our needs as a race in terms of evolutionary progression.

The system must change and our children are the torch-bearers of the next generation who will help lead the way toward change, growth and conscious expansion because it is time for our world to change, to adapt and to grow to suit the needs and demands of the evolving energy of our planet.

These bright children do not need to adapt to fit into a stale and dysfunctional system which does not fulfill the needs of our planet and its growth, therefore we must stop over-diagnosing them with mental illness, unnecessarily drugging them; and start disciplining them, otherwise they will not be able to do the work they were born to do and our planet will suffer as a result.

Society needs our children. We must embrace them and their differences by learning to adapt to their demands and follow their lead. We must begin to change the way we think and the way we do things so that we are able to flow with the shifting tides of change. If we do not, I fear that humanity, and our world will suffer greatly as a result.

Dr. Ashleigh Stewart Msc.D.

The children are precious and are a gift to the world. It is time to respect children, recognize who they really are, honor them and love them UNCONDITIONALLY instead of allowing them to be judged, defined and labeled in negative ways by a system that they are unable to fully resonate with.

Chapter 11

Understanding Karma & Responsibility

KARMA DEALS WITH the law of cause and effect where everything that you do, say, think or feel creates a circumstantial experience as a result. In other words, whatever you say and think, and however you treat yourself and others will create an effect on you or them and depending on the intention behind what you have done, the result will have a positive or negative effect in yours or the other person's life.

In essence the law of karma is about responsibility. Children can learn from an early age about taking responsibility for their choices and actions; and how what they do creates their life circumstances and affects others' lives too.

Karma is a central component of my kid's yoga and mindfulness classes. The reason is because the center of a child's power is knowing that he has the power to create his own life and influence others through thought, action and word.

Children these days should be taught to understand that they are powerful beyond measure, and can be taught to use that power constructively by reining it in, then guiding it with discipline and structure in a safe environment.

The exercises here in this book are all centered in the theme of karma; and educating the child about how he uses his mind and body to affect the life he lives, how he feels in his body and in his own space, as well as in his relationship with others through consideration and responsibility.

Chapter 12

Five Minutes to Breathe

"When you own your breath, nobody can steal your peace" - Author Unknown

PRANAYAMA IS A science which refers to the channeling and expansion of our life force and energy. The word *Pranayama* comes from two Sanskrit words: the first is *prana* which means the fundamental life force that flows through all things; and *yama* which means to control. Pranayama is, therefore channeling or controlling the life force through the breath.

Working with the breath is a fundamental component of any well-rounded wellness plan; it doesn't only apply to yoga. The breath is our most precious gift providing us with a constant stream of life sustaining oxygen and prana. We know that prana is the vital life source of energy in yogic terms, however, you may also know prana as *Chi* which is how it is referred to in Chinese medicine.

The breath serves as an anchor upon which we can focus our attention. Through the breath we can come back to our center and

49

feel grounded and calm in the midst of any stressful situation. It is also the connection which helps the mind and body working in harmony as one.

When mind and body is connected we feel a sense of being stable, present in the moment and as a result more capable of handling challenging situations. I believe that when we take in a full, long, deep breath during moments of anxiety and fear we are reclaiming our body, our mind and our ability to root into the situation and handle it, as opposed to feeling scattered, confused and powerless.

Breath work is a perfect tool for children because it is simple - and like most of the strategies I am offering in this book - it can be done anytime, anywhere. Try the following breathing exercises with your child. Each exercise is designed to help during challenging situations. Try them all and then use each one when applicable. Eventually, after habitual practice, your child will naturally know which breathing exercise to practice when he is alone in real life situations which trouble him.

Breath 1. Hot Air Balloon Breath - CALM

Hot Air Balloon breath is a traditional belly breath and is useful for calming your child and reducing anxiety by instantly slowing down the stress response in the body.

Ask your child to sit down and begin talking long deep breaths into his belly. Ask him to place his hands on his belly while visualizing his belly filling up like a big hot air balloon that's about to lift off up into the air.

Ask your child to imagine that he is in the balloon basket ready to take off and that his anxiety, stress, fear or uncertainty is the very stuff which fires up the balloon to lift it into flight.

Now ask him to imagine himself exhaling his fiery breath up into the balloon, inviting him to feel more relaxed and calm as he allows all the negative feelings to leave his body.

Finally the balloon is up in the air and the fiery breath gives way to a cool peaceful one as the balloon stabilizes into its soaring glide and your child is finally relaxed. Ask him to allow his breath to remain relaxed, effortless and natural.

Leave him for a few moments to enjoy peaceful moments of silence, imagining himself soaring through the air. There he is above all the world in his balloon feeling relaxed, light and carefree.

Breath 2. Snake Breath - CLEANSE

Snake breath is not only a lung cleansing breath, it is also effective in helping children calm down and self-regulate. When practicing snake breath, explain to your child that she is going to relax like a snake, and that the goal is to see how long you she can hiss while allowing her lungs to empty out completely. This eliminates stale air and any germs that might be hanging out in there. Explaining the exercise this way makes it more appealing to the child as a game, not just an exercise so she is likely to be more enthusiastic about joining in.

Ask your child to sit down in a chair or cross-legged on the floor. Then ask her to breathe in deeply through her nose, and then out through her mouth making a long hissing – SSSSSS- sound.

With each hissing snake exhalation, ask her to try to hiss even slower to make the exhale last even longer. This part of the exercise is great for slowing children down both mentally and physically.

Younger kids love the use of props to make breath work more appealing and engaging because they are not working with the movement of their bodies which can make the work more confusing or difficult to concentrate on. My own daughter loves to use her stuffed snakes as 'breathing buddies' to help her relax and focus on her breath work. Your child can work with a breathing buggy too and with these sorts of fun props you will likely have a more successful time practicing breath work with your child.

Repeat this exercise as often as you feel your child needs to enjoy its benefits. If your child claims she is feeling dizzy, do not worry. It just means there is a change in the blood flow happening and oxygen is entering the brain. This can be stabilized by her taking in a deep breath and holding her breath for three seconds while nodding her head down, chin tucked into her chest.

Breath 3. Bumblebee Breath - FOCUS

Bumblebee breath is similar to *Bhramari* in traditional yogic Pranayama practice. This breath reins in energy and helps focus attention inward.

Ask your child to sit down comfortably with his hands on his knees. Younger children can also use their arms to imitate bee wings flying. This movement is effective in stimulating the lymph glands under the armpit enhancing immunity!

Ask your child to now breathe in deeply through his nose, then on the exhale use his mouth to make a buzzing sound just like a bee - BZZZZZZZ.

To enhance the exercise, you can add vibrating lips on the third breath, then a humming sound on the fifth breath. When the child reaches the humming breath, you can ask him to put his thumbs in his ears and fingers over his eyes to close off his external sense receptors. This action helps turn the focus of the child's attention inward; to his inner world and private senses.

There is a comforting feeling of safety which emerges from this exercise; as well, it has a calming effect on the mind and body. Bee breath is particularly effective for helping children manage the behaviors which come of feeling very scattered and disorganized because it helps them focus.

Breath 4. Bunny Breath - INVIGORATE

Bunny Breath is always a favorite with children, especially younger ones. It is a useful exercise for when children are very upset and can't find their breath. Bunny breath helps children connect to their exhalation so that they breathe instead of hyperventilating. As well, it is an invigorating breath which helps children to amplify their energy while they are feeling low.

To begin, ask your child to think about how bunnies breathe and ask him to show you how he thinks it is done.

Now ask your child to take three quick sniffs through his nose like a bunny. If he likes he can hold up his hands like a bunny would hold his paws, then let out one extended exhalation through the nose. Tell them (the younger ones) to pretend they're sniffing carrots! A stuffed bunny is also a cute addition to the exercise to join in as your child's breathing buddy.

Repeat the breath as for as long as your child needs to feel relaxed, centered and invigorated.

Breath 5. Alternate Nostril Breath - COORDINATION

Alternate Nostril is a technique which is beneficial for older kids as it is more of an advanced breath work exercise. This technique is known as *nadishodhana* in traditional pranayama practices and aims to balance the energy and flow of *prana* throughout the body.

Alternate nostril breath engages both hemispheres of the brain throughout the exercise which helps with coordination and balancing the function of the nervous system.

Yogis believe the right nostril is connected with the left hemisphere of the brain and the left nostril with the right hemisphere of the brain. By alternating the breath through each nostril, it induces a state of harmony between the two hemispheres, encouraging relaxation, stress reduction and is also helpful in eliminating insomnia and improving concentration.

Ask your child to sit comfortably and relax, taking in a few deep breaths. Using the thumb of the right hand lightly block off the right nostril and exhale through the left. Then take a full inhalation through the left nostril keeping the right side closed.

Ask him to release his thumb from the right nostril.

Now using his the pinky finger of the right hand (he can fold the ring, middle, index finger gently in towards the palm of his hand so they are out of the way as shown in the image above), gently close off his left nostril and exhale through the right. Then ask him to take a full inhalation through the right nostril keeping the left side closed, releasing the baby and ring finger from the right nostril. Repeat the same steps above for five rounds until your child feels a sense of peace, calm and centeredness.

Because of the deeply relaxing effect this exercise has on the body and mind, it is beneficial to practice it last thing at night before bed. The effect of the exercise helps to induce a deep, quality, long-lasting sleep. Sweet dreams!

Chapter 13

Five Minutes to Move

"It is easier to build strong children than broken adults" – Unknown

MOVEMENT IS A fundamental part of any children's yoga and mindfulness practice. Movement helps children to feel grounded and present in their bodies. Excess energies are released and the production of endorphins are stimulated which helpschildren feel happy and enjoy better periods of rest and sleep.

Many of the adults I have suggested yoga to are apprehensive claiming that the child will not sit still or pay attention. In many cases, yes, it can be challenging to keep children engaged in yoga, however, just like adults sitting still, focusing and paying attention during yoga and meditation is a discipline which children can learn.

If you feel apprehensive about starting your child in a yoga program, remind yourself of these two points:

1. Children can develop the skills and the discipline required to sit still and follow instruction as long as the activity is fun, interesting and engaging.

2. Do not judge or underestimate what your child can and cannot do. Give them the space to figure things out for themselves and you might just be amazed.

In the Five Minutes to Move section of this book we will explore two types of yogic body movements for children:

1. *Asana*, the Sanskrit word for a static posture.
2. *Vinyasa, the* Sanskrit word describing the flow of movements coordinated with breathing.

In this book, I would like to introduce you to a series of fundamental *asana* and mini *vinyasa* that I personally like to use in my work with children. These are the exercises which I feel are most efficient to help children combat feelings of stress and anxiety; induce feelings of trust, safety and relaxation. They also help develop skills in focus and concentration, balance and coordination and lastly, confidence through a feeling of strength, flexibility and stamina.

These postures can be used one at a time during moments of heightened stress and anxiety or even during low energy moments. Read through the descriptions of the exercises and their effects and benefits and as you become familiar with each one, over time and with practice you will instinctively start to know which one your child needs and when. The goal is for your child to become so accustomed to practicing yoga that he will begin to practice these postures himself when he feels the need. As suggested, at first you can encourage your child to choose a few postures to help himself; then with time and practice you will eventually feel confident enough to create mini-partner yoga sequences or games together with your child and siblings to make yoga more fun and engaging.

On a final note before I introduce the postures, here's a rule of thumb I like to stick by: when it comes to children, less is always more. When it comes to yoga, it is not the length of time you practice that achieves the results; it is the consistency of how often you practice. As I mentioned in the first chapter of this book, five minutes of practice a few times a day creates way more effective results than an hour of practice once a week. The reason for this is because the brain and the mind respond to habitual behaviors. Through habitual repetitive behaviors, the brain creates new neural pathways of information that will be communicated between the brain and the body. The more you instill the idea of calmness, focus and concentration as a repetitive behavior, the sooner it will become second nature to the child to feel this way because the brain has rewired itself to respond to messages of relaxation and calmness as opposed to nervousness and anxiety. To encourage consistent, non-resistant yoga practice try to not to force children into long-winded repetitive sessions. Instead choose one or two poses when necessary and the brain will be more receptive to the introduction of yoga. This will create a habit of being used to yoga and the child's brain will respond more readily to the new behaviors and feelings you are instilling in the child's consciousness. Then, for them, it becomes second nature.

Asana 1. Downward Facing Dog - PERSPECTIVE

Downward Facing Dog is a favorite pose amongst children and adults alike because it offers a full back body stretch from the toes to the fingertips and provides us with an opportunity to look at things from another angle, that of being upside down. This posture teaches kids perspective, and that there are alternative ways of looking at things, doing things and approaching things. Because Downward Facing Dog puts kids into an inverted position it instantly slows them down, increases blood flow to the brain which helps stabilize the function of the nervous system and releases excess energy.

With younger children you can make this asana fun by adding the following variations:

- Add sound by voicing doggie sounds - "Woof woof".
- Add a dog tail by asking the child to extend a leg from the floor into the air and shake it from side to side mimicking a dog's tail wagging.

- You can 'walk the dog' by asking your child to bend one knee, lifting the heel off the floor then alternate to the other leg. Keep alternating the movement from leg to leg creating the rhythm of a dog walking.

Asana 2. Tree Pose – FOCUS

Tree Pose is a balancing pose which requires the child to balance on one foot, with his palms together overhead and his other foot placed against the inner thigh of the leg holding his weight. Tree Pose is excellent for developing balance and focus, as well as calming and connecting your child's mind and body to function as one. Ask your child to focus a spot on the wall and lift the foot while remaining balanced. Watching their spot helps the child maintain steadiness, focus and balance.

Any static posture in yoga where a part of your body is suspended requires that the brain activity slow down, the flow of mental chatter must cease to support the suspension of the limb that is lifted, as well as balance the body which is rooted to the floor. As soon as your mind wanders off into thoughts not related with what the body is doing you will lose balance and topple over. Try it and you will see!

Vinyasa 3. Windy Palm Tree - STABILITY

Windy Palm Tree is similar to Tree Pose, however it is an extension of the static posture of the tree into a flowing mini *vinyasa* where the child sways side to side in unison with his breath while keeping his feet rooted in one place. While the child is centered with her spine straight, ask her to inhale then stretch to the right, ask her to then exhale then come back to center with a straight spine. Ask her to inhale then stretch to the left, then exhale back to straight spine at center. Follow the same flow of movement coordinated with breath for several rounds.

I like to teach children this pose as it teaches them about the importance of stability. I explain that in real life the roots of a tree always remain rooted into their foundation, the ground which supports them, but often the wind will blow and shake the tree from side to side. Life is like that too. Sometimes, something will happen that shakes us out of our comfort zone and change things up, but it does not mean that our feeling of stability needs to be compromised. We can still feel grounded in our bodies with a strong sense of self awareness. This mini *vinyasa* is a great way to begin teaching children about life and how the 'winds of change' will blow and bring them to new experiences, however they need not lose their identity or feeling of stability as a result. Stability is an inner state of being, regardless of the circumstances or environment you find yourself in. This is a fundamental and seriously empowering lesson for children to take with them into their lives as they grow into adults.

Asana 4. Warrior 2 – CONFIDENCE

The Warrior Two asana inspires strength, bravery and valor. The Warrior Two represents what it means to be resilient & persevere in the face of challenges. Use this asana to invoke courageousness in your child's life. This inner strength when harnessed will help your child to overcome the stresses and pressures he faces every day.

Physiologically, this posture helps build core and leg strength. It invokes a deep sense of being grounded and rooted as most of the energy of this pose is contained in the legs.

Ask your child to stand with his feet together at the top of his mat, then take a giant step back with one foot.

His front toes will continue to point forwards, as his back toes turn out to the side. Ask him to make sure his front heel is in line with the arch of his back foot.

His shoulder and hips should remain open towards the same direction his back toes are pointing.

Now help him lift his arms out to the sides, wrists in line with shoulders, parallel to the floor.

Now ask him to inhale, then on his exhale ask him to bend his front knee until it is aligned directly above his ankle with his shoulders staying directly over his hips and look out over his front hand. Hold for several deep long breaths.

Vinyasa 5. Rag Doll - RELEASE

This is a fantastic pose for loosening up tense children and they will love it just because of its name! 'Ragdoll' helps release tension in the neck and shoulders, stretches leg muscles and relieves stress. It also calms the mind and makes the child feel refreshed and relaxed.

Ask your child to stand up straight with his arms extended above her head. On an exhale, ask her to bend her body forward allowing her arms to fall toward the floor.

With slightly bent knees ask her to gently sway her head and arms from side to side like a floppy ragdoll. After a few minutes, ask her to slowly roll back up to standing position.

Asana 6. Mountain - REFLECT

Mountain Pose is the foundation for all of the standing postures in yoga and is one of the first poses we learn as beginners. It helps to improve posture, develops a feeling of being grounded and solid with stability and confidence. I like to invite children to close their eyes and turn their attention inward to reflect on what their energy levels, thoughts and feelings are like. Through awareness they can change their feelings to more positive ones.

To strike Mountain Pose ask your child to stand still, nice and tall with a straight spine and belly pulled in. Feet should be hip width apart and shoulders relaxed, down away from the ears. Arms can remain by the child's side or they can bring their hands together in front of their heart in 'Namaste Mudra' or 'Prayer Pose'. Let them remain in Mountain Pose as long as they need to feel grounded and to reflect on their inner world.

Vinyasa 7. Cat & Cow - STRETCH

The 'Cat & Cow' vinyasa is effective in aiding the function of the digestive system and for strengthening and lengthening the spine. As well, it stimulates the nervous system while it increases the circulation of blood in and around the spine to the brain. Cat and Cow is a perfect mini vinyasa to use with children as it is a simple exercise which coordinates breath with movement and sound.

Ask your child to come onto all fours and spread her fingers wide like they are cat paws. Encourage him to round his back upwards on an exhalation while tucking his chin into his chest, and tailbone is tucked under. Ask him to look towards his belly button, and "meow" like a cat. Now ask him to inhale and arch his back downward, letting his belly drop toward the floor. As he lifts his chin and chest towards the sky he can "moo" like a cow. Move back into Cat Pose and "meow" even louder! Repeat about five rounds of this vinyasa.

Asana 9. Upward Facing Dog Pose - TRUST

This asana is a classic heart-opening pose. When the child's chest cavity is open without feeling tight and restricted he can begin to develop deeper feelings of openness and trust within himself, his relationships and the world around him. This asana also works to make the spinal cord strong and long. This asana not only opens the chest but stretches it too, making it helpful for decreasing stress level and helping with symptoms associated with asthma.

Ask your child to lie on the floor face down with his palms on the ground under his shoulders, keeping his elbows locked in beside his body. Ask him to use a little strength and push his body up from head to waist looking slightly upwards. Breath remains normal and relaxed. His legs should be straightened with tops of his feet resting on the ground, and knees should be straight and locked. He can stay in this asana for 25-30 seconds, or as long as he can while building strength in his arms.

Dr. Ashleigh Stewart Msc.D.

Variations for younger children

Younger children enjoy this pose too and I like to call it 'Puppy Pose' by adding a little breath work to make it fun and engaging for younger children. Follow all the same directions above, however, ask the children to open their mouths wide, let their tongues hang out and make panting breaths just like an excited puppy would. This is a great breathing exercise to develop the throat chakra energy center in the body which encourages healthy expression and communication. As well, it is effective physiologically for clearing the throat and lungs of any germs, helping to boost immunity and health.

Asana 10. Child's Pose - REST

The child's pose is my favorite restorative pose. It helps release stress and induces feelings of safety and nurturing. This pose is called child's pose as it mimics the position of the fetus while in utero. I believe this pose reignites the subconscious memories of safety and the warmth we felt from our mother while nestled in-utero.

Physiologically, this asana stretches the muscles of the lower back, hips and thighs. In addition, this pose has a calming effect on the central nervous system.Kneel down on the floor with your big toes touching together.

Ask your child to sit back on her heels, with knees hip-width apart. On an exhale, ask her to bend forward to bring her chest to rest on top of her thighs. She can stretch her arms out in front or tuck them in by her sides. Encourage her to relax and breathe deeply, holding this pose for one to five minutes.

Asana 11. Savasana - SLEEP

Savasana means 'corpse pose' in Sanskrit. The meaning of this pose speaks for itself! It is in my opinion the most important pose of all in any well rounded yoga practice.

Savasana is a time to rest, relax and let go into stillness and quietude. It can be very difficult for some children to let go and relax quietly while remaining awake, others even feel insecure and vulnerable just lying there so I invite them to use their breathing buddy to support them with feelings of fear and vulnerability. The breathing buddy allows the children to relax by giving them an anchor to focus on.

Ask your child to lie back, relax and bring his focus to the breathing buddy and notice how his buddy rises and falls with the rhythm of his breath. Then invite your child to let go and try to relax. Explain that when he lets his body and mind relax, he is giving his body the space it needs to rest, recuperate and heal itself into wellness and strength. It is also important to remind your child that rest and being still is equally as important as being active and always doing things. Society teaches us from early on that it is more appealing to be active and we are considered to be more successful the more we do, and as true as that may be, we also need to teach our kids we will not be successful if we are burnt out, tired and feeling overwhelmed and spent. Teach your child the importance of taking restful breaks often. It is one of the greatest gifts you can give him.

Chapter 14

Five Minutes to Meditate

"While meditating we are simply seeing what the mind has been doing all along."– Allan Lokos

MEDITATION HAS SIGNIFICANT mental and physical health benefits for children. It is great news that it is becoming more commonly practiced in schools. Many schools now have yoga as part of their curriculum and are offering short meditations in class. My first experience of meditation was when I was around eight years old in my gym class at primary school. We only did it that one time but I never forget how good I felt during and after the exercise, and so continued to try it when I was alone in bed at night.

Practicing meditation shows children can be more relaxed, more focused and more able to cope with the school day. Research has shown that meditation increases serotonin levels in the brain, and growth hormones are released which repair body tissue and cells. Meditation also helps to lower heart rate, blood pressure, increase blood circulation, boost immunity, improve sleep quality, create mental and emotional wellness and induce a state of calmness and inner peace.

If your child is new to meditation, it is beneficial to introduce the practice of meditation slowly as to avoid resistance and restlessness. Like adults, a child's brain needs time to adjust to being still and quiet for an extended period of time, and meditation is a discipline which is slowly cultivated over time with lots of patience.

The following exercises are designed to help cultivate different states of being within your child from rest to imagination! They are designed to be easy and fun to practice. The 'Lemon Face' will require more time than the others because the child is required to focus on and work with each different part of the body. I hope you enjoy meditating with your child. I know I do.

Meditation 1. Rainbow Body - REST

My own children love the 'Rainbow Body' meditation. It is a modification of the chakra balancing meditation I teach my adult students during chakra yoga classes made especially for children.

This easy meditation is a great exercise to do with your kids at night before they fall asleep as it will really help them to relax and unwind before bedtime. It is also fun and helps children to develop their creative visualization and their imagination. Start with a couple of minutes to begin with, slowly building up to five or seven minutes. Choose one color first, then perhaps two or three, slowly building the children's meditation practice up to the whole rainbow of color. Remember, let them be the guide and have patience. Practice makes the master! You can teach this meditation exercise to your children and they will love it! But first, try it for yourself so you know how it feels. Here goes!

Find a comfortable place to lie down and stretch your body through your fingers to your toes to stretch out any tension knots. Then wiggle your arms and legs, your fingers and toes, and roll your head and wiggle your nose.

Now, relax and lie still and quietly. Get as comfortable as possible because we will be here for a few minutes. Inhale deeply through your nose and imagine the air flooding in through your nose, filling your chest, your lungs and all the way into your belly, making it big like a balloon. Hold your balloon belly for a few seconds then exhale deeply making a big 'huff'. (Repeat this breathing exercise for three to four breaths).

Let your breathing come back to a natural rhythm and feel your body relaxing more and more, becoming heavier and heavier as if you are sinking into a soft and squishy marshmallow floor.

Now imagine a bright red light glowing right at the bottom of your belly. The light gets brighter and warmer and begins to spread throughout your body more and more with every breath. It goes from your belly down through your legs to your feet, and then up through your arms and hands into your head and all around you until you are completely filled, and surrounded by a glowing bright red light. The red light makes you feel secure and strong in your body.

Imagine a bright orange light glowing in your belly just under your belly button. The light gets brighter and spreads down your legs to your feet, through your arms and hands, and all the way up to the top of your head and all around your body with every breath. You are now glowing a bright orange light. The orange light makes you feel inspired, creative and able to express your feelings.

Imagine a bright sunny, yellow light now glowing just above your belly button. It is getting brighter and brighter as you breathe, and is spreading throughout and around your body. You are glowing a warm and golden yellow color. The yellow light is warm and you feel confident, happy and energized.

Now, imagine a green light glowing in the middle of your chest, near your heart. As you inhale the green light gets brighter and spreads throughout and around your entire body and you are glowing a bright green light. The green light radiates with love and compassion. You are filled with so much love for yourself and others that your heart just might burst now! Imagine that green light expanding out to all your friends and family who you love so they can feel love too.

Now imagine a cool blue light in your throat. The blue light gets brighter with each breath. See the bright blue light spreading through your body until you are glowing blue all over. The blue light makes you feel confident about speaking your truth, about who you are and what you believe in. The blue light also helps you to listen to, and respect other people's truth too. You are feeling relaxed, calm and happy.

Now imagine an indigo light glowing on your forehead, between your eyebrows. Indigo is a color like the dark blue sky at night. See the indigo light getting brighter, spreading through your head and down your whole body right to the tips of your fingers and toes and all around you. The bright indigo light brings you clarity, helping you to see things clearly and to believe in your dreams and deepest feelings and intuitions.

Now imagine a bright purple light glowing right at the top of your head. The purple light is getting bigger and brighter as you breathe. It spreads through your whole body, into your belly, your arms and hands and all the way down your legs right to the tips of your toes until you are glowing deep purple inside and out. This purple light is connected to the light and energy that is in everything, and everyone around you. The natural world, the trees and flowers and all the planets and stars in the sky and connected to this light. This light represents the infinite and eternal wisdom that is in us all. You feel safe and deeply happy and content in this light.

Now imagine all of the colors joining together in a big bright rainbow above your head. The rainbow gets brighter and extends all around you with its glowing arc of rainbow light. As you inhale, imagine the rainbow colors entering your body and filling it completely until your body and the rainbow become one in this rainbow of light. Rest in the rainbow, you are protected and safe in this light.

If you are not going to bed to sleep, it is time to come back to the rest of your day. Start to wiggle your fingers and toes and become aware of the weight of your body on the floor. Take your time to slowly open your eyes and when you are ready, you can sit up.

If you are going to sleep, stay in the rainbow of light; it will bring you sweet dreams and happy thoughts and feelings. When it is time to wake up in in the morning you will feel healthy, energized, happy and refreshed, ready to take on the day ahead.

Now that you are familiar with this meditation please share it with your child. At first he she might seem impatient and fidget, but with perseverance, you will eventually get her used to the idea of relaxing for an extended period of time. Remember her brain has to rewire itself for this so give her time and space to adjust.

Meditation 2. Lemon Face - RELEASE

This exercise will help your child learn how to relax when he or she is feeling anxious or stressed. It can also help reduce physical problems such as stomachaches and headaches, as well as improve sleep. The technique involves tensing and then relaxing different muscles in the body. This can help your child learn the difference between being tense and feeling relaxed.

The key is to start practicing this exercise during times when your child is already relaxed so that when he does feel anxious, he accepts the exercise easily.

Helpful tips for a successful practice:

- Set aside 15 to 20 minutes to complete this exercise.
- Find a place where you and your child can complete this exercise without being disturbed.
- Older children often prefer to do this exercise on their own. Give them space to find a quiet place to practice alone.
- When reading the instructions, speak slowly with a calm and soothing voice. Pause after each instruction to allow your child time to carry it out.
- Use age appropriate vocabulary for older children, changing the word from *tummy* to *stomach* as an example.
- Make sure your child is not squeezing too hard. He should feel tightness in his muscles, but not pain· Ask him to squeeze each muscle for five seconds before relaxing.

When you are ready and your child is comfortable with his eyes closed, slowly read the following instructions:

"Inhale and hold your breath for a few seconds then breathe out. Take another deep breath through your nose and imagine your tummy is a big balloon filling up with air. Hold your breath then let it go imagining that the air in the balloon is escaping. Focus now on your body and notice how it feels.

"Let's now focus on your legs. Stretch out your legs in front of you and point your toes. Squeeze the muscles in the top of your legs really tight. "Now squeeze the muscles in the bottom of your legs really tight. Hold it till I count to five. One, two, three, four, five: now relax your legs and let out a big sigh, ahhhhhh. Relax all the muscles in your legs till your legs feel nice and soft and floppy. Notice how heavy your legs feel. Take in a deep long breathe and release it with a big sigh, ahhhhhh.

"Now, make a fist with your left hand and squeeze tight. Imagine that you are holding a lemon and you are squeezing out all the juice. Feel how tight your hand and arm is and hold it till I count to five. One, two, three, four, five: now relax your hand. Your hand is relaxed. Notice how it feels when it is relaxed.

"Now make a fist with your right hand and squeeze your lemon tight again and squeeze all the juice out. Feel how tight your hand is and hold it for five counts. Relax your hand and take a deep breath and let it go with a big sigh, ahhhhh.

"Now stretch your arms out in front of you like you are reaching out to grab something, stretching as far as you can. Hold the stretch for five counts One, two, three, four, five, then relax with a big sigh, ahhhhh. Let your arms fall to your sides and notice how relaxed your arms feel. Inhale deeply and let it go with a big sigh ahhhhhhh.

89

"Now focusing on your shoulders, shrug them up to your ears as tight as you can - tight tight tight, then relax. Take in a long deep breath and breathe out with a big sigh, ahhhhh

"Now, pull in your tummy muscles as far as you can then hold it One, two, three, four, five, then relax all the muscles in your tummy and blow it out like a big balloon: One, two, three, four, five; then relax. Now take a deep breath and let it out with a big sigh, noticing how your tummy feels when it is relaxed.

"Finally, imagine you have just drank a whole glass of the sour lemon juice you squeezed earlier. It tastes so sour! Wrinkle up your face as much as you can and purse your lips together. Notice how tight the muscles in your face feel. Hold it for One, two, three, four, five; then relax. Now open your eyes wide and your mouth and jaw as wide as you can. Hold for One, two, three, four, five; then relax. Now take a deep breath and breathe out with a big sigh, ahhhhh.

"Now relax your whole body pretending you are a rag doll. Try to relax all the muscles in your body and pay attention to how good it feels to be relaxed. Take a deep breath and hold it; then breath out with the last big sigh, ahhhhh. When you are ready, you can slowly open your eyes. What an amazing job you have done relaxing your body and mind while being so patient. Good job!"

After some practice and your child has learned to tense and relax her whole body consciously, the next step is to practice relaxing the body and mind without the step of tensing up first. This is an effective strategy your child can easily turn to in a wide range of situations at home and at school.

Ask your child to take a deep breath, then exhale while mentally repeating the word "relax" to himself while letting his whole body go limp like a rag doll. If your child needs to, he can work with several breaths, each time letting his body become looser and more relaxed after each breath.

The goal is to help your child develop a quick strategy to help him or her relax in any challenging or stressful situation. Good luck!

Meditation 3. Magical Flying Carpet Ride - IMAGINE

"Imagination is the space where the soul roams free" - Dr. Ashleigh Stewart

This is an exhilarating meditation exercise for children to cultivate and expand their imagination and unleash their inner sensory awareness. Imagination is a fundamental aspect of not only dreaming about, but actually creating the life of one's dreams and during childhood our imagination is at its best. Unfortunately through time and with the implementation of the conditioning of the system in our rational world, children are often taught to believe that their imagination is senseless, just a dream, not real and a lot of 'codswallop' - a term I often heard myself as a child. Luckily, I was strong enough to never let go of my dreams and never stopped using my imagination as I knew deep inside that my imagination gave me insightful glimpses into who I really was, what my gifts were and what the purpose of my life was. Unfortunately, this is not the case for most children who end up allowing the system and what adults tell them is true to overrule the insights they catch in their imagination. Imagination is the fire which ignites the pursuit of making all dreams come true in life. Please do not let your child lose or extinguish this fire, help him to cultivate it no matter how 'out there' his visions may be.

Ask your child to lie down in a comfortable place and invite her to take in three long, deep breaths, exhaling after each with a sigh and allowing herself to fall deeper and deeper into a state of relaxation.

Ask her to turn her attention to the inner pictures and thoughts in her mind. Ask the child to imagine that her mind is like a huge movie theatre screen and she is watching her thoughts and images of her mind on the large screen. The more she focuses on the screen, the more engaged she becomes until finally she is in the movie of her mind.

Ask her to now imagine that in the movie of her mind she is walking in a beautiful lush green meadow. It is a lovely summer's day and the sun is high in the blue cloudless sky and it is hot. Begin to engage all her senses in her mind by inviting her to feel the warmth of the sun on her skin, smell the scent of the green grass, and hear the sound of the birds singing and the bees buzzing as they fly in the meadow. She can even engage the sense of taste by picking a plump blackberry from a nearby bush to eat. Mmmm! The idea here is to invoke all of the child's senses to use in the inner world of her imagination so that everything is as real as can be. Remember the mind doesn't distinguish what is a real physical experience, or what is not; it just sees the information we feed it through our sensory experience so as far as the mind is concerned, the experience the child is seeing in her mind in this meadow is real.

Now you ask your child to walk slowly in the meadow toward an object she sees a little further away. When she reaches the object she discovers it to be a beautiful, fluffy, colored rug. The child can imagine the rug to be whatever color she likes. She realizes that this rug is hovering slightly above the ground and starts moving toward her. She is apprehensive, yet curious and so takes her seat on this rug.

The rug is a magical, flying carpet and has the power to fly and carry your child wherever she pleases. Invite the child to ask the rug to fly and begin building her adventure in her own mind. She might like to fly to a country she has never seen, or visit a friend in a faraway place. She might want to visit an exotic country to see wild animals she has only ever heard of in books or seen on television. She may like to visit a distant relative. Regardless, ask her to build the adventure in her own special way by really engaging all her senses as if it is really happening. Allow her to have space and a few minutes of silence to do so.

After her quiet time to fly has passed, invite her to slowly start directing the flying carpet back down into the meadow. She can come back into the movie of her mind at any time to visit the meadow and find her very own magical, flying carpet at any time she wants to embark on a vivid adventure in her mind.

Ask her to step off the carpet and lie in the grass. Gently ask her to now start to notice the feeling of her body on the floor, or wherever she is lying in the room. Feel her breath entering and leaving her body as she breathes and then slowly awaken back into consciousness in the room by gently stretching and sitting up when she is ready.

You can ask her if she would like to share her adventure with you. If she is shy about it don't force her to. You can also let her write in her journal about her experience or draw pictures to express what she has seen and felt. Never try to rationalize, criticize or tell your child she is wrong for imagining what she did as this is one way in which we start to strip children of their sense of self-esteem and conviction. We do not want to them to doubt who they are and what their dreams are. We want them to believe in them and watch them grow into becoming self-assured adults brimming with a sense of conviction.

Meditation 4. Sunny Golden Light – ENERGIZE

> *"Keep your face always toward the sunshine and shadows will fall behind you." - Walt Whitman*

The energy of the sun is active, and masculine in its nature. It is the perfect source of energy that provides vitality, life force and optimism. Any time you notice your child feeling sluggish or low on energy, try this bright sunny meditation to zest things up again. I like this exercise because it is very short and it can be done at any time anywhere and need not be done lying down.

Ask your child to get comfortable either lying or sitting down. Invite him to take three deep, long breaths, exhaling with a sigh and relaxing more with each breath.

Now ask the child to imagine that a big bright sun is shining in a blue sky over him. The sun is sending down a big bright beam of golden energy to him. Ask him to notice the feeling of the warmth and energy of the light as it shines onto his skin. Now ask him to imagine the sunlight is entering his body, spilling throughout his whole body and around him until he is surrounded in a big bright sphere of sunlight. Give him a few moments to bask in his light sphere.

When five minutes has passed, ask the child to slowly allow the light to fade, and ask him to return to consciousness in his physical body in the room. Taking in a few, nice, long, deep breaths have him wiggle his fingers and toes, stretch out fully and open his eyes. He should be ready to face the rest of the day with energy, optimism and enthusiasm.

Meditation 5. Birthday Cake Candle - CONCENTRATE

This is another simple-to-do-anytime-anywhere exercise which helps to sharpen your child's mind by instilling in him or her the ability to concentrate through the act of concentrating on a fixed object. This exercise is done, however, by imagining there is a candle burning that she can see in her own mind.

I particularly like this meditation for children who display behaviors such as a short attention span and inability to focus on an activity as it trains them to concentrate for longer periods of time. Even if they do not particularly like an activity they are involved in, such as a subject or activity at school. Regular practice of this exercise can help them learn how to manage their attention and focus on a fixed point or event for longer periods of time regardless of how they feel about it. It is also effective for children who tend to daydream as it grounds the attention down to a fixed point and trains the mind to be sharp.

Ask your child to sit upright in a chair or on the floor. We want her to sit up with a nice straight back to keep the circulation of blood flowing nicely between the brain and the spine during this exercise. We want the body to be awake and alert during the exercise to train the mind to be focused and concentrated while in a state of relaxation and stillness. The exercise is not nearly as effective is she lies down as the body and mind may become too relaxed and less focused.

Next ask her to imagine she is at her own birthday party and she is feeling happy and excited. It is time for birthday cake so ask her to imagine that her cake is sitting in front of her on the table and the candles are burning brightly. Ask her to instead of blowing the candle out, pick one of them and focus on the slow glow of the flame as it dances in its own space. Ask her to notice the way the flame sways in the air from side to side, and see the different colors that make up a flame from the glowing light orange color to a darker orange, and the blue and black in the center.

Explain to her that before she can blow the candle out she must watch it burn, melting down slowly in its own heat. Give her a few moments to silently watch the candle burning in her mind and ask her that when the candle almost burns down to touch the cake, blow them all out and make a special wish.

When she is done she can open her eyes and come back into consciousness in the room with you, feeling relaxed yet energized, centered and focused.

Congratulate your child on her hard work and focus as this can be a tough exercise for children in the beginning; however, with all of these exercises in this book through time, effort, patience and determination eventually everything you (and your child) are learning here will become like second nature and that is the goal. We want your child's second nature to be a restful, focused, creative and happy nature as opposed to being stressed, afraid, misunderstood and confused.

Chapter 15

Five Minutes to Mindfulness

MINDFULNESS INVITES US to become aware of what is already true to us in each individual moment. Becoming mindful teaches us how to be unconditionally present with whatever is happening, regardless of what it is.

The goal of mindfulness for children is not directed toward trying to make them become someone else. The practice of mindfulness provides children with the opportunity to become more present with who they are, just as they are with full acceptance and without judgment, or what is right or wrong.

When children learn to become really present with who they are, they begin to see glimpses of inner wisdom which encourages them to stay true to who they are, how they feel and to emerge from the unnecessary suffering that results from trying to be someone they are not. Children can learn to *be* with what *is*, and then build upon developing their emotional skills, behaviors and knowledge from there.

Mindfulness is not only effective for dealing with negative situations, it can be brought into positive experiences as well.

Believe it or not, some children have difficulty staying present with feelings of happiness when they are used to feeling (and being viewed as someone) 'negative,' particularly when they are diagnosed with a behavioral or mental disorder. I experienced this with my own daughter Tiffany while she was going through the difficulties at school that I mentioned at the beginning of this book. I feel that when children are in an emotional state like this, it robs them of their childish essence and childhood innocence.

These children can have such a hard time accepting happy experiences that they end up turning them into something negative, for example worrying that the feeling isn't real because it is unfamiliar. Often they will unconsciously feel that their happiness won't last, or that something will go wrong. Like adults, children too can become so accustomed to living with anxiety that they are unable to simply let their feeling of happiness be.

When we allow our children to have the space they need to slow down and remain mindful in the present moment, they are able to show up in their own lives. The opportunity to feel great doesn't escape them because we are allowing them to be who they are, instead of forcing them to be someone they are not, or wishing that things could be different in our relationship with them.

Here are some of my favorite exercises to cultivate the different components of mindfulness in our children individually. Many of these exercises can be done with partners or in a group which helps build a community spirit with teamwork, respect and co-operation. I hope you enjoy participating in the exercises with your child too!

Mindfulness Exercise 1. Self-Love Circle - POSITIVE SELF IMAGE

Take a few moments to sit in a circle with your child and other family members. Take a few moments to relax and ask everyone to close their eyes, take three nice deeps breaths and think about something that they like about themselves and a quality that makes them special.

Take turns to go around the circle asking each one and to share it out loud.

This can be a very challenging exercise for both children and adults alike. The reason is because as a society in general we are taught to focus on our flaws so as to improve them; but not our strengths. It will not make a child idle about striving for greatness when he focuses on what he likes about himself. On the contrary, it will instill feelings of confidence, self-assuredness and the inner power to believe he can accomplish his dreams. Focusing on what his flaws are all the time will not motivate him to become his best self for the right reasons. Let him be his best for himself, not to prove himself to others. Focus on self-love first.

Mindfulness Exercise 2. Choosing Positive Focus - GRATITUDE

A great practice for children, and yourself, is to create a gratitude list every day, preferably in the morning. The reason that this is an effective mindfulness exercise is because it shifts a person's focus from what is lacking to what is already abundant in their life.

Focusing on gratitude affects everything, especially in children because they are so easy to mold. It is a simple way to help a child becomes a more positive person, a more productive person and a better sibling. No-one is perfect, but I do believe that focusing on gratitude makes people feel better about themselves and their life and there is nothing wrong with that!

You can make a gratitude list with your child by investing in some nicely colored pens and paper, as well as a little time each day.

Take a few moments to settle down with your child. Ask her to take a few deep breaths and close her eyes. Ask her to meditate for a few moments, thinking about all of the things she feels grateful for.

Then ask her to open her eyes, choose the color of paper and pen she likes and simply begin writing a list of all the things she feels grateful for in her life.

Mindfulness Exercise 3. Blessings Bags - EMPOWER

A Blessings Bag is similar to a gratitude list; however, it comes in handy when a child is feeling particularly down, anxious, afraid or stressed.

The idea of the Blessings Bag is to have a ready-made tool kit which the child can reach for during challenging times. She can use it to make herself feel better when she might not have the capacity to sit down and have the focus and concentration required to make a gratitude list.

The bag serves as a reminder of all of the things we have to feel happy about and grateful for in our life and can be a quick way to turn feelings of fear and anxiety into comfort and happiness. A tool like this empowers a child with that capacity to re-direct his thoughts and feelings from negative to positive with the focus on little blessings to focus on from his own life.

The Blessings Bag can be made out of a brown paper lunch bag which the child designs himself, in any way he likes. Give your child little scraps of different colored pieces of paper upon which he can write different words or notes to himself which serve as reminders of the things in his life which makes him feel grateful and happy.

He can fill the bag with as many notes as he likes, then store it in a safe place so that when he feels down or afraid he simply has to reach into his bag and pick out a little note of positivity for an instant mood lift!

Mindfulness Exercise 4. Mandala's – INDIVIDUALITY

Mandala is a sanskrit word that stands for 'sacred circle'. A mandala is a spiritual and ritual symbol representing the universe.

For this exercise you can spend time with your child studying the different forms of mandala that exist in nature. Some examples to look at are petals forming around their center, snowflakes, sliced oranges and kiwi fruit that grow outward from a single seed. Ask your child to reflect inward and think of her own individuality and her life as a representation of her own personal Universe.

You can incorporate movement into this exercise by working through some yoga postures such as 'Tree Pose' which mimic nature, forms that grow outward from a singular seed -a center - just like a mandala does.

Ask your child to close her eyes and spend some quiet time reflecting on aspects of herself and her life that are special, unique and sacred to herself as an individual. Then give her a piece of paper with a circle drawn in the center and ask her to draw a symbol of herself in the center of the mandala, and then surround herself with drawings or words that represent the different aspects of her life. Or she can simply fill the circle with drawings of things which have an extra special relevance or importance to her in her own life.

Here are a few examples drawn by children in classes I taught in the past. I hope you enjoy them. It is always interesting for children to express what is contained in their mind and heart.

Mindfulness Exercise 5. The Wishing Jar - IMAGINATION

The use of props like this 'Magical Wishing Jar' that children help to make for themselves helps to invoke imagination and inspire little minds to start working toward making little dreams into big realities!

To make this wishing jar into a reality you will need to collect some supplies: a mason jar; some decorative stickers; glitter; sequins and little buttons, jewels or anything else that will look pretty when shaken in the jar.

All you have to do to make the jar is decorate the jar with the stickers, then fill it about a quarter full with the glitter, sequins and jewels, then top it up with some water then close the lid tight! It is a very easy, yet fun project to take part in with your child.

If you want to make the wishing jar even fancier you can add a drop of food coloring to the water to make it brighter.

When the jar is ready you can ask your child to shake up the jar and make a wish while she watches the glitter swirl around in the water!

I like to use the wishing jar mindfulness tool with my own children every day as it helps to keep their minds focused on their dreams and desires with optimism, and when children are in a state of optimism they will work harder and feel capable of making their dreams come true!

Mindfulness Exercise 6. Understanding Diversity - ACCEPTANCE

A favorite mindfulness exercise that I like to do with larger groups of children is to use of breathing buddies to illustrate diversity. The different breathing buddies promote mindfulness and awareness around inclusion and emotional acceptance because our buddies are all unique with different skin tones, appearances, body types and emotional expressions.

Using breathing buddies to illustrate differences between each other in terms of body shape, skin tone, and even moods is an effective way to introduce children to diversity and that it is OK to be different. I always like to explain to children that what makes us unique makes us special. What makes us different makes us unique.

Ask your child at home to reflect for a few moments on what it is that makes him unique? If you have different stuffed toys or dolls at home you can use as buddies to help enhance the exercise that is great.

Ask your child to draw or write down all the things about him that makes him different from others, therefore unique.

You may want to spend a little time discussing what he has drawn or written on this paper as this can be a quite emotionally moving exercise for children and having a conversation can give him some comfort and validation in terms of what has come up for him. Keep in mind however: do not try to correct or judge your child in any way; simply listen to him and understand that what he is expressing is *his* truth, not yours.

Of course it is helpful to guide your child through feelings of inadequacy, or insecurity but correcting the way they see who they are or trying to convince them to change your way, may only add to a child's confusion. Sensitivity, and getting your own view out of the way is an effective approach in this exercise.

Mindfulness Exercise 7. Identifying & Understanding Feelings – EMOTIONAL INTELLIGENCE

Emotional intelligence is an important aspect of mindfulness for children. When children are able to understand and relate to their feelings and why they are feeling the way they do in response to their environment then they can then begin to learn to regulate their feelings, responses and reactions to everyday situations.

One thing I would like to mention before discussing this exercise further is that none of this is about identifying feelings as being 'right' or 'wrong'. It is simply about educating children about identifying their feelings; and showing him ways in which he can be better equipped to regulate and manage his emotions in a healthy and consistent way without resistance or force. All of this cannot be accomplished until the child has developed a degree of self-awareness though his emotions.

The easiest way to begin teaching children about their feelings is to try to have children identify how they are feeling and match it with facial expressions. This is the best way to begin teaching children about the connection between the body, mind and emotions and that how we feel about ourselves affects our bodies too.

Another easy way to have children begin understanding about the nature of different feelings is to match them up with a color. Colors stimulate different types of feelings within us and children in particular are typically very sensitive to the energies of color.

For example, my own daughter always tends to match feelings of anxiety with yellow, green with feeling calm and relaxed, blue as feeling unhappy and red as feeling very angry. My son on the other hand relates to blue as a feeling of calmness, yellow as happiness and purple as feeling relaxed and sleepy.

You can begin by educating your child about his emotions by inviting him to sit one day with you during a quiet and relaxed part of the day. Gather some paper and pens in a variety of colors and begin to ask your child if he is able to list the different types of emotions he feels and match them up to a color.

Examples of basic emotions that children can easily identify are:

- Happiness.
- Sadness.
- Loneliness.
- Boredom.
- Frustration.

- High Energy (Anxiety).
- Low Energy (Depression).
- Fear.

You can now begin teaching your child to start mapping his feelings by identifying them with different types of facial expressions and body responses. Examples are folded arms; downward chin; slumped shoulders; etc. Ask your child to draw his interpretation of those bodily expressions of feeling in colors of his choice.

Sometimes it can be hard for children to identify with just one feeling at a time, as they may be feeling an array of feelings at once. For example: you may be moving to a new home in a new part of town and as much as your child is so happy to be living in a new house, he is also worried about changing schools. I like to refer to these emotional states as *kaleidoscope feelings* meaning there are several different feelings happening at once. Feeling this way can be extremely confusing for a child but exercises like emotional mapping can help him to break down each feeling, understand it and know that it is okay to feel in different ways about any situation and that different feelings may even overlap.

In terms of teaching your child to emotionally regulate as a response to identifying his feelings, you can refer to any of the previous exercises in the earlier sections of this book. Select appropriate exercises based on how your child is feeling and reacting specifically to what is happening for him now, and he will learn to use his exercises as tools to manage and eventually regulate his feelings on his own. Keep in mind that some exercises may work better than others for your child. All children are different but let him be the guide. He must feel good about what he is doing in order for him to be able to adapt to working with mindfulness exercises because if he is resistant then it will not work. Resistance is a form of fear and where there is fear there is no trust, and where there is no trust there is fear. Work slowly with your child and let him begin to trust you and that this work can be useful for him to help himself in the long run. It is not supposed to be a chore, but a fun way for him to start changing the way he sees and feels about himself so he can better adapt to and respond to the world around him effectively.

Mindfulness Exercise 8. Butterfly Yoga - ADAPTING TO CHANGE

Little yogis can make magical butterfly wands, or practice butterfly themed yoga postures to help them to understand life changes and transformation. Butterfly themed exercises can teach children that change is often necessary, and that regardless of where they are they can always grow to become more and reach their goals when they are willing to adapt to, and move with the winds of change.

Adults and children respond differently to change, and while children, especially young ones, thrive on routine and familiarity, it can become very disruptive for them emotionally and mentally when sudden changes occur.

Here are a few examples of situations of where children may have trouble adapting to change:

- Moving home.
- New decoration/renovation in the home.
- Changing school.
- Family separation.
- New class teacher.
- Friends moving away.
- New clothes.
- Loss of a pet or loved one.
- Transitioning from daycare to school.
- New caregivers.

You can ask your child to reflect on situations where the change has been challenging or made for a tough transition. Tell them a story of how butterflies were once caterpillars, and how they must spend a period of time in a dark cocoon they create for themselves while they are turning into a butterfly.

If you have a butterfly wand, the child can hold the wand while she is thinking of situations which have been hard for her. If not, you can ask her to pretend she is a caterpillar who has just woven his cocoon and is waiting there till the change has occurred and ready to emerge as a butterfly.

After a few minutes of reflection you can now ask your child to think about all the good things which occurred as a result of the change that happened in her life. Examples could include that a new school brings new opportunities for friendships. A new home means a new bedroom! The loss of a pet means there is a chance to give a home to another animal who desperately needs one.

It is not about undermining the child's feelings of uncertainty toward change, but to help her see the alternative positive aspects which can occur in light of new things happening in life.

Now ask your child to pretend that she is a butterfly by sitting upright, bringing the soles of her feet together and flapping her knees up and down like a butterfly. Invite her to imagine that she has emerged from the darkness and uncertainty of the cocoon as a beautiful and majestic butterfly ready to embark upon new adventures in her new life as a butterfly!

Chapter 16

Children are a Promise that the World can go on!

"A baby is an inestimable blessing." - Mark Twain

BABIES ARE STILL being born, our population continues to grow and the world keeps turning. The mere fact that babies are being born means that Souls are still choosing to reincarnate into this world, this physical plane, and it is not the end of our life cycle here in this world.

I came across the following quote by Carl Sandburg, in his book 'Remembrance Rock,' published in 1948: *"A baby is God's opinion that life should go on"*

To me this quote was inspiring, motivating, encouraging and above all, affirming of the fact that children are a sacred and divine gift to our world. They provide the key to open the doorway into a future which promises growth into wisdom, awareness and higher consciousness.

It is time to guide our children toward embracing their differences and for us adults to view the challenges they provide us with as opportunities to grow. It is time to let children be who they were born to be, to express their unique individual nature and live the life they were born to live.

I have dedicated my life's work to all the world's children, to help them discover and express all that they have chosen to bring into our world to lead us toward growth, awareness and the collective evolution of our planet, and our race as a result. It is time to honor and respect children for the gifts they have to share with us and start helping them to fulfill their mission, and their destiny instead of hurting them, confusing them and giving them mind-altering drugs for alleged behavioral disorders at the drop of a hat.

Let's endeavor to help our children by slowing down, spending time and giving them space within which they can thrive and grow. Let us find the compassion and unconditional love in our hearts to embrace them, accept them and allow them to express who they are and the gifts they have brought to share with us. Bless them.

Chapter 17

Your Own Notes & Reflections

"There are only two lasting bequests we can hope to give our children. One of these is roots, the other, wings." – Johann Wolfgang von Goethe

NOW IT IS your turn to write! Please use the space on these empty pages that follow to fill with important notes about your observations and reflections on the progress of your mindfulness practice with your child.

Dr. Ashleigh Stewart Msc.D.

Notes and Reflections

Notes and Reflections

Notes and Reflections

Notes and Reflections

Notes and Reflections

Notes and Reflections

Notes and Reflections

Notes and Reflections

About The Author

Dr. Ashleigh Stewart Msc.D.
Author, Metaphysical Counselor, Therapeutic
Yoga Instructor & Holistic Health Expert

ASHLEIGH'S STUDIES STARTED in the field of Psychology however; the scientific approach to the study of the mind did not satisfy her interest in the mind/body connection, and so she switched her focus toward to the holistic approach of spiritual psychotherapy, holistic biochemistry and metaphysical science.

Ashleigh eventually was awarded her doctorate in metaphysical counseling, where her concentration was therapeutic yoga, during which she studied the effects of stimulant drugs upon children, and therapeutic yoga as a natural approach to treating children diagnosed with ADHD.

Ashleigh is a certified yoga instructor of the 'Bali Method of Therapeutic Yoga' and has been teaching yoga and meditation to children and adults for over 10 years.

Ashleigh's experience with children extends beyond teaching yoga. She a family childcare in her home during the years she stayed at home after having had her own two children. She is a certified in Infant & Child First Aid & CPR certified in Fundamentals of Family Childcare, Introduction to Science & Physical Education for Family Child Care and Nutrition Basics for Children. As a hobby, she teaches a community program in the local after school club where she bakes with the children.

Visit the author's websites at www.ashleighstewart.com and www. littlelighthouseyoga.com to obtain 25% off the purchase of an online program, or product with coupon code FIVEMINUTES.

CPSIA information can be obtained
at www.ICGtesting.com
Printed in the USA
LVOW07s0433100817
544445LV00001B/11/P